STEM K-5

THE MATH CHEF

OVER 60 MATH ACTIVITIES AND RECIPES FOR KIDS

Joan D'Amico
Karen Eich Drummond, R.D.

Illustrations by Tina Cash-Walsh

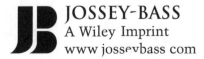

JOSSEY-BASS
A Wiley Imprint
www.josseybass.com

Library of Congress Cataloging-in-Publication Data

D'Amico, Joan,
    The math chef : over 60 math activities and recipes for kids / Joan D'Amico, Karen Eich Drummond ; illustrations by Tina Cash -Walsh.
        p.   cm.
    Includes index.
    Summary: Relates math and cookery by presenting math concepts and reinforcing them with recipes. Provides practice in converting from English to metric system, multiplying quantities, measuring area, estimating, and more.
    ISBN 0-471-13813-4 (pbk. : alk. paper)
    1. Cookery—Juvenile literature. 2. Mathematics—Juvenile literature. [1. Cookery. 2. Mathematics.] I. Drummond, Karen Eich. II. Cash-Walsh, Tina, 1960- ill. III. Title.
TX652.5.D348   1997
641.5'123—dc20   96-22143

Printed in the United States of America
FIRST EDITION
PB Printing   15 14 13 12

Dedicated to the premise that math can be fun, practical, and delicious!

CONTENTS

PART 2 ARITHMETIC

ABOUT THIS BOOK

Math goes with cooking like peanut butter goes with jelly. Recipes in cookbooks are chock-full of numbers and measurements, from the amount of each ingredient needed to the number of servings the recipe makes and so on. For example, to make chocolate chip bars, you measure some ingredients, such as 1 cup of margarine, and weigh some ingredients, such as 12 ounces of chocolate chips. You also count some ingredients, such as 2 eggs. You can use multiplication to double your chocolate chip bar recipe, or use division to cut the recipe in half.

The Math Chef will help you learn more about math and cooking in new and tasty ways. The first section, "Discovering the Kitchen," covers the basics about kitchen tools, cooking skills, and safety rules. Read it carefully before you do any of the Math Activities or try any of the recipes. The next fourteen chapters cover the math topics of English and metric measurements; length; volume; weight; temperature; multiplication; division; estimation; fractions; percents; area of squares and rectangles; and diameter, radius, circumference, and area of circles.

Each chapter begins by introducing and explaining a different math concept, followed by a Math Activity involving cooking or exercises and problem-solving. (Answers to the activities can be found at the back of the book.) The last part of each chapter includes several delicious recipes that allow you to apply and practice the math skill you learned in the chapter.

Each recipe is rated according to how much cooking experience is required. The easiest recipes, marked with one chef's hat (called a *toque*), require no previous cooking experience. Intermediate recipes, with two chef's hats, require some cooking experience. Pro recipes, with three chef's hats, require the most advanced cooking skills.

Always be sure you have an adult to guide you when the activity or recipe asks you to use the oven, the stove, electrical appliances, or a sharp knife.

easiest

intermediate

pro

These recipes also:

- list the time you will need to make them, the kitchen tools you'll need, and the number of servings each recipe makes

- use easy-to-find ingredients and standard kitchen equipment

- are kid-tested and kid-approved

- emphasize wholesome ingredients

At the end of the book, you'll find a glossary and sections on nutrition and food safety, including an explanation of how to read a food label. There's also a chart listing the nutritional values of all the recipes in the book.

So put on your apron, wash your hands, roll up your sleeves, and get ready to become an expert Math Chef. We hope you have as much fun learning, cooking, and eating as we did writing this book for you!

Joan D'Amico
Wayne, New Jersey

Karen Eich Drummond
Yardley, Pennsylvania

DISCOVERING THE KITCHEN

THE MATH CHEF'S TOOLS OF THE TRADE

baking pan

colander

cutting board

biscuit cutter

cookie sheet

electric blender

electric mixer

Let's take a close look at the cooking equipment in your kitchen. These are the basic tools you'll need to prepare the recipes in this book. Any kitchen tools that are used in only one or two recipes are described within those recipes.

baking pan   A square or rectangular pan used for baking and cooking foods in the oven. The most common sizes are 9-inch × 13-inch and 8-inch square.

biscuit cutter   A round outline, usually made from metal, used to cut biscuits from dough.

colander   A large perforated bowl used for rinsing food and draining pasta or other foods.

cookie sheet   A large rectangular pan with no sides or with half-inch sides, used for baking cookies and other foods.

cutting board   Made from wood or plastic, cutting boards provide a surface on which to cut foods.

electric blender   A glass or plastic cylinder with a rotating blade at the bottom. A small motor in the base turns the blade. The blender has different speeds and is used for mixing, blending, grinding, and pureeing.

electric mixer   Two beaters that rotate to mix ingredients together. Used for mashed potatoes, cake batters, and other mixing jobs.

grater   A metal surface with sharp-edged holes used for shredding and grating foods such as vegetables and cheese.

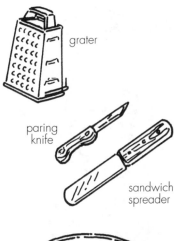
grater

knives:

- **paring knife**   A knife with a small pointed blade used for trimming and paring vegetables and fruits and other cutting jobs that don't require a larger knife. (Most recipes in this book call for a knife. You will find the paring knife works well in most situations.)

paring knife

sandwich spreader

- **peeler**   A handheld tool that removes the peel from fruits and vegetables.

- **sandwich spreader**   A knife with a dull blade that is designed to spread fillings on bread.

- **table knife**   A knife used as a utensil at the table.

layer cake pans   Round metal pans used to bake layers of a cake.

layer cake pan

measuring cups   Cups with measurements (½ cup, ⅓ cup, etc.) on the side, bottom, or handle. Measuring cups that have spouts are used for liquid ingredients. Measuring cups without spouts are used for dry ingredients such as flour.

measuring cup

measuring spoons   Used for measuring small amounts of foods such as spices. They come in a set of 1 tablespoon, 1 teaspoon, ½ teaspoon, and ¼ teaspoon.

measuring spoons

microwave dish   A dish that can safely be used in the microwave oven. The best microwave dishes say "microwave safe" on the label. Don't use metal pans, aluminum foil, plastic foam containers, brown paper bags, plastic wrap, or margarine tubs in the microwave.

mixing bowl

mixing bowls   Round-bottomed bowls used for mixing and whipping all kinds of foods. Depending on the amount of ingredients, a large, medium, or small bowl may be used.

muffin tins   Metal or glass pans with small, round cups used for baking muffins and cupcakes.

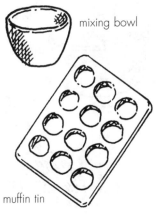
muffin tin

frying pan

saucepan

pastry blender

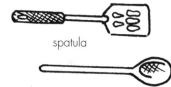
rolling pin

rubber spatula

spatula

wooden spoon

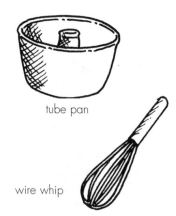
tube pan

wire whip

pans:

- **frying pan** (also called a sauté pan)   Used for cooking foods, such as hamburgers or onions, in hot fat.

- **saucepan** (also called pot)   Used for general stovetop cooking, such as boiling pasta or simmering a sauce.

pastry blender   A group of stiff wires attached to both ends of a handle. It is used, with a rocking motion, to blend butter or margarine into flour and other dry ingredients to make a dough.

rolling pin   A wooden or plastic roller used to flatten items such as pie crust and biscuit dough.

rubber spatula   A flat flexible rubber or plastic tip on a long handle. It is used to scrape bowls, pots, and pans and for **folding** (a gentle over-and-under motion) ingredients into whipped cream or other whipped batter.

spatula   A flat metal or plastic tool used for lifting and turning meats, eggs, and other foods.

spoons:

- **teaspoon**   A spoon used for measuring. Also the name for the spoon normally used as a utensil at the table.

- **wooden spoon**   Used for mixing ingredients together and stirring.

tube pan   A metal cake pan with a center tube used for making angel food cakes, bundt cakes, and special breads.

wire whip   Used especially for whipping egg whites and cream.

wire rack   Used for cooling baked goods.

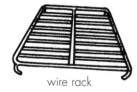
wire rack

COOKING SKILLS

Chefs need to master cutting and measuring skills and the basics of mixing and stovetop cooking. Here are the skills you will be practicing as you try the recipes in this book.

CUTTING

Foods are cut before cooking so that they will look good and cook evenly. Place the food to be cut on a cutting board and use a knife that is a comfortable size for your hand. To hold the knife, place your hand on top of the handle and fit your fingers around the handle. The grip should be secure but relaxed. In your other hand, hold the item being cut. Keep your fingertips curled under to protect them from cuts. (See the "Safety Rules" section of this chapter for more on how to cut safely.)

Here are some commonly used cutting terms you'll need to know.

chop   To cut into irregularly shaped pieces.

dice   To cut into cubes of the same size.

mince   To chop very fine.

slice   To cut into uniform slices.

Grating and shredding are also examples of cutting.

grate   To rub a food across a grater's tiny punched holes to produce small or fine pieces of food. Hard cheeses and some vegetables are grated.

shred   To rub a food across a surface with medium to large holes or slits. Shredded foods look like strips. The cheese used for making pizza is always shredded.

chopped

diced

sliced

minced

grate

shred

Equivalents
1 tablespoon = 3 teaspoons
1 cup = 16 tablespoons
1 cup = 8 fluid ounces
1 quart = 2 pints
1 quart = 4 cups
1 quart = 32 fluid ounces
1 gallon = 4 quarts
1 stick butter or margarine   = ½ cup = 8 tablespoons

MEASURING

Ingredients can be measured in three different ways: by counting (six apples), by measuring volume (½ cup of applesauce), or by measuring weight (a pound of apples).

To measure the volume of a liquid, always place the measuring cup on a flat surface and check that the liquid goes up to the proper line on the measuring cup while looking directly at it at eye level.

To measure the volume of a dry ingredient, such as flour, spoon it into the measuring cup and level it off with a table knife. Do not pack the cup with the dry ingredient— that is, don't press down on it to make room for more— unless the recipe says to. You'll learn a lot more about measuring in Part 1 of this book.

MIXING

There are all kinds of ways to mix! Here are definitions of the most common types.

beat   To move a utensil back and forth to blend ingredients together.

cream   To mix a solid fat (usually margarine or butter) and sugar by pressing them against a bowl with the back of a spoon until they look creamy.

fold   To move a utensil with a gentle over-and-under motion.

mix   To combine ingredients so that they are all evenly distributed.

whip   To beat rapidly using a circular motion, usually with a whip, to incorporate air into the mixture (such as in making whipped cream).

whisk   To beat ingredients together lightly with a wire whip until they are well blended.

beat

fold

whip

STOVETOP COOKING

There are different ways to cook on your stove. Here are descriptions of cooking methods you will be practicing as you try the recipes in this book. Because it is easy to get burned while cooking on the stove, see the "Safety Rules" section of this chapter.

boil   To heat a liquid to its boiling point, or to cook in a boiling liquid. Water boils at 212°F. You can tell it is boiling when you see lots of large bubbles popping to the surface. When a liquid boils, it is turning into steam (the gaseous state of water). Water can't get any hotter than 212°F; it can only make steam faster. Boiling is most often used for cooking pasta.

boil

simmer   To heat a liquid to just below its boiling point, or to cook in a simmering liquid. You can tell a liquid is simmering when it has bubbles floating slowly to the surface. Most foods cooked in liquid are simmered. Always watch simmering foods closely so that they do not boil.

simmer

steam   To cook in steam. Steam has much more heat and cooks foods more quickly than boiling water does. Steaming is an excellent method for cooking most vegetables.

pan-fry   To cook in a pan over moderate heat in a small amount of fat. Hamburgers are an example of a food that can be pan-fried.

sauté   To cook quickly in a pan over medium-high heat in a small amount of fat. Vegetables, especially onions, are often sautéed in oil to bring out their flavor and brown them.

sauté

CRACKING AND SEPARATING EGGS

It is best to crack an egg into a clear glass cup (such as a measuring cup) before adding it to the other ingredients. That way, if the egg smells bad or has a red spot, you can throw it out before the egg goes in with the other ingredients. An egg with a red spot is safe to eat, but is usually thrown out because of its appearance. You should also remove any pieces of eggshell from the egg before adding the egg to the other ingredients.

Sometimes you will need to separate the egg yolk from the egg white for a recipe. To do this, crack the egg over an egg separator and a bowl. Make sure you get the yolk in the middle. The whites will drain out into the bowl. If you don't have an egg separator, you can separate an egg by cracking it over a bowl, keeping the yolk in one half of the shell. Carefully pass the egg yolk from one half of the shell to the other without letting it break until the whites have all fallen into the bowl.

SAFETY RULES

The kitchen can be a safe, or a very dangerous, part of your home. What's dangerous in your kitchen? Sharp knives, boiling water, and hot oil are a few things. Always check with an adult before trying any of the recipes. Talk to him or her about what you are allowed to do by yourself and when you need an adult's assistance. And always follow these safety guidelines.

AROUND THE STOVE AND OVEN

- Get an adult's permission before using a stove or oven.

- Don't wear long, baggy shirts or sweaters when cooking. They could catch fire.

- Never turn your back on a frying pan that contains oil.

- Never fry with oil at a high temperature.

- Don't spray a pan with vegetable oil cooking spray over the stove or near heat. Oil will burn at high temperatures, so spray the pan over the sink.

- If a fire starts in a pan on the stove, you can smother it by covering it with the pan lid or pouring baking soda on it. Never use water to put out a fire in a pan with oil—it only makes a fire worse.

- Always use pot holders or wear oven mitts when using the oven or handling something that is hot. Make sure your pot holders are not wet. Wet pot holders transmit the heat from the hot item you are holding directly to your skin.

- Don't overfill pans with boiling or simmering liquids.
- Open pan lids away from you to let steam escape safely.
- Keep pan handles turned away from the edge of the stove. Knocking against them can splatter hot food.
- Stir foods with long-handled spoons.
- Keep pets and small children away from hot stoves and ovens during cooking. (Try to keep them out of the kitchen altogether.)

USING ANY APPLIANCE

- Use an appliance only if you know exactly how to operate it and you have permission from an adult.
- Never operate an appliance that is near the sink or sitting in water.
- Don't use frayed electrical cords or damaged plugs and outlets. Tell an adult.

USING A MICROWAVE OVEN

- Use only microwave-safe cookware, paper towels, paper plates, or paper cups.
- Use pot holders or oven mitts to remove items.
- If a dish is covered, make sure there is some opening through which steam can escape during cooking.
- When taking foods out of the microwave, open the container so that steam escapes *away* from your hands and face.
- Prick foods like potatoes and hot dogs with a fork before putting them into the microwave.
- Never try to cook a whole egg in the microwave—it will burst!

USING A KNIFE

- Get an adult's permission before using any knife.
- Always pick up a knife by its handle.
- Pay attention to what you're doing!
- Cut away from the body and away from anyone near you.

- Use a sliding, back-and-forth motion when slicing foods with a knife.
- Don't leave a knife near the edge of a table. It can be easily knocked off, or a small child may touch it.
- Don't try to catch a falling knife.
- Don't use knives to cut string, or to open cans or bottles, or as a screwdriver.
- Don't put a knife into a sink full of water. Instead, put it on the drainboard, to avoid cutting yourself.

PART 1

MEASURING

What kinds of things do you measure in the kitchen? Well, to make an apple pie, you measure:

- length (a 9-inch pie pan)
- volume (a cup of sugar)
- weight (a pound of apples)
- temperature (350°F)
  - time (45 minutes)

Now you know what measures to take to make an apple pie! But there's a lot more ahead to measure for a Math Chef!

CHAPTER 1

HOW MANY GRAMS IS A POUND OF POTATOES?

If you were sent to buy potatoes at the store, you would probably buy them weighed by the pound. The pound is a unit of weight in the English system of measurement, the measurement system commonly used in the United States. The most common units of measurement in the English system are: the foot to measure length, the cup to measure **volume** (the amount of space an object takes up), and the pound to measure weight.

In almost every other country besides the United States, however, you would buy potatoes weighed by the gram. The gram is a unit of weight in the metric system of measurement. Most of the world uses the metric system. The most common units in the metric system are: the meter to measure length, the liter to measure volume, and the gram to measure weight. You're probably already familiar with the metric system. For example, although milk in the United States is sold by the quart, soda usually comes in a 1- or 2-liter bottle.

The following charts compare English and metric units of length, volume, and weight.

Length	
English	Metric
1 yard (yd)	.9 meters (m) (almost 1 meter)
1 foot (ft)	30 centimeters (cm)
1 inch (in.)	2.5 centimeters
1 inch	25 millimeters (mm)

Volume

English	Metric
1 quart (qt)	946 milliliters (almost 1 liter)
1 cup (c)	240 milliliters (ml)
½ cup	120 milliliters
¼ cup	60 milliliters
1 tablespoon (Tbsp)	15 milliliters
1 teaspoon (tsp)	5 milliliters

Weight

English	Metric
2.2 pounds (lb)	1 kilogram (kg)
1 pound	454 grams (g)
½ pound	225 grams
¼ pound	113 grams
1 ounce (oz)	28 grams

You can use these charts to **convert** (change) measurements from English to metric units. To find the answer to the following problem:

1 pound of potatoes = ? grams of potatoes

Look at the chart on weight, which tells you that:

1 pound of potatoes = 454 grams of potatoes

It's hard to get an exact conversion between the English and metric systems, however. When we don't need an exact answer, we just try to get close. This is called **estimating.** For example, although ½ pound is half of one pound, 225 grams is not exactly half of 454 grams. This is because we have estimated the metric units.

MATH ACTIVITY **METRIC MANIA**

Materials

3 charts above

pencil

notebook

Procedure

1. Change each of the following measurements of length from English to metric units.

    a. 1 yard = ? meters licorice

    b. 1 foot = ? centimeters submarine sandwich

    c. 1 inch = ? millimeters ravioli

2. Change each of the following measurements of volume from English to metric units.

    a. 2 teaspoons = ? milliliters vanilla extract

    b. ¼ cup = ? milliliters half-and-half

    c. 1 quart = ? milliliters skim milk

3. Change each of the following measurements of weight from English to metric units.

    a. 1 ounce = ? grams chocolate bar

    b. 1 pound = ? grams ground turkey

    c. 2.2 pounds = ? kilograms hot dogs

Check your answers in Appendix A.

FAST MEAL RECIPES

In each of these healthy fast meal recipes, one ingredient is shown in **boldface** type. You'll need to change those measurements from English to metric units. Check Appendix A for the answers when you're finished.

Baked Crunchy Chicken Bites

Making your own chicken nuggets is not only easy, it's fun, too!

Ingredients

vegetable oil cooking spray

¼ cup flour

¼ teaspoon black pepper

⅛ teaspoon cayenne pepper

1 egg

2 tablespoons = ? ml 2% milk

2 dozen snack crackers

4 boneless chicken breast halves

Steps

1. Preheat the oven to 400°F.

2. Spray the cookie sheet with vegetable oil cooking spray. Set it aside.

3. Place the flour, black pepper, and cayenne pepper in one of the plastic bags. Seal the bag and shake it to mix the ingredients well. Set it aside.

4. In the medium bowl, whisk the egg and milk together.

5. Put the crackers in the second plastic bag and seal the bag or close with a tie. Crush the crackers by rolling the rolling pin over the bag until the crackers are crumbly. Put the crushed crackers in the small bowl.

6. On the cutting board, use the paring knife to cut the chicken into bite-size pieces, about 1 inch by 1 inch.

Time
10 minutes to prepare
plus
10 to 12 minutes to cook

Tools
cookie sheet

2 1-gallon resealable plastic bags

medium bowl

wire whip

small bowl

rolling pin

cutting board

paring knife

oven mitts

Makes
6 servings

*If you prefer,
you can use your
favorite cold cereal
rather than crackers
to make crumbs to
coat the chicken.*

7. Put the chicken pieces into the first plastic bag with the flour mixture. Seal the bag or close with a tie, and shake to mix. When all the pieces are dusted with flour, remove the chicken from the bag.

8. Dip the chicken pieces two-by-two into the egg mixture and then into the cracker crumbs.

9. Place the chicken pieces in a single layer on the sprayed cookie sheet.

10. Bake for 10 to 12 minutes or until golden brown. Remove cookie sheet from oven using oven mitts.

Superquick Stromboli Slices

You can make your own stromboli in no time, using frozen bread dough from the supermarket that you've thawed. Stromboli has the same ingredients as pizza, only it's rolled up.

Time
10 minutes to prepare
plus
20 to 25 minutes to cook

Tools
cookie sheet

rolling pin

small bowl

fork

pastry brush

oven mitts

knife

Makes
8 servings

Ingredients

vegetable oil cooking spray

1 loaf frozen white bread dough, thawed overnight in refrigerator

¼ pound = ? grams ham, thinly sliced

⅛ pound turkey salami, thinly sliced

¼ pound pepperoni, thinly sliced

⅓ pound part-skim mozzarella, grated

¼ pound cheddar cheese, grated

½ cup Parmesan cheese

1 egg

Steps

1. Preheat the oven to 350°F.

2. Spray the cookie sheet with vegetable oil cooking spray.

3. On a clean surface, use the rolling pin to roll out the bread dough into a rectangle 14 inches by 16 inches.

4. Layer the ham, salami, and pepperoni slices onto the bread dough, leaving a 1-inch border all around.

5. Sprinkle the mozzarella, cheddar, and Parmesan cheeses evenly over the meats.

6. Roll the dough up by starting with a shorter side and rolling the dough toward you. Tuck in the ends.

• • • • •

Turkey salami is made from turkey but tastes like regular salami. It generally has less fat than salami made from pork or beef.

• • • • •

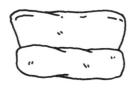

7. Beat the egg with the fork in the small bowl.

8. Use the pastry brush to brush the top of the bread dough with the beaten egg.

9. Place the stromboli on the cookie sheet with the seam side down. Bake for 20 to 25 minutes until golden. Remove the cookie sheet from the oven using oven mitts.

10. Slice the stromboli into 1-inch slices and serve.

Lean & Mean Open-Face Turkey Burger

Turkey is a popular substitute for ground beef in making burgers because it is lower in fat.

Ingredients

1   medium yellow onion

1 pound = ? grams ground turkey

1½ tablespoons Worcestershire sauce

½ teaspoon garlic powder

4   hamburger buns

4   lettuce leaves

4   slices tomato

4   tablespoons reduced-fat mayonnaise or favorite salad dressing

Steps

1. Preheat the oven to 350°F.

2. Remove the outer skin of the onion. On the cutting board, use the knife to slice the onion in half, then cut each half into three pieces. Chop the onion.

3. In the bowl, use the wooden spoon to combine the onion, ground turkey, Worcestershire sauce, and garlic powder.

4. Shape the meat mixture into four burgers.

5. Place the burgers on the rack in the roasting pan and bake for 20 minutes.

6. While the burgers are cooking, open up four hamburger buns. Place 1 lettuce leaf, 1 tomato slice, and 1 tablespoon of mayonnaise or your favorite salad dressing on each bun.

7. Use oven mitts to remove the pan from the oven. Use a spatula to place each burger on a bun.

Time
15 minutes to prepare
plus
20 minutes to cook

Tools
cutting board

paring knife

large mixing bowl

wooden spoon

roasting pan with rack

oven mitts

spatula

Makes
4 burgers

• • • • •
Yellow onions are a favorite for cooking. A medium yellow onion is about 2 inches long. White and red onions are also available.
• • • • •

···· McQuick Oven Fries ····

Time
10 minutes to prepare
plus
25 minutes to cook

Tools
peeler

cutting board

paring knife

medium bowl

cookie sheet

oven mitts

Makes
6 servings

• • • • •

Kosher salt is
coarser than
regular salt.

• • • • •

Instead of the traditional deep-fat fried
potatoes, try these fries cooked in the oven.

Ingredients

4 baking potatoes

1 tablespoon = ?
milliliters oil

vegetable oil cooking spray

1 teaspoon kosher salt

Steps

1. Preheat oven to 425°F.

2. Wash and scrub the potatoes. Peel the potatoes and place them on the cutting board.

3. Use the paring knife to slice each potato into ¼-inch slices. Cut each slice into 4 long, thin pieces.

4. Place the fries in the bowl and toss with the oil.

5. Lightly spray the cookie sheet with vegetable oil spray.

6. Place the fries on the sheet and bake for 25 minutes or until they are lightly golden brown.

7. Use oven mitts to remove the cookie sheet from the oven. Dust the fries with salt and serve.

Choose your favorite ice milk or frozen yogurt
flavor to make a healthy milkshake.

Time
5 minutes

Tools
electric blender

2 glasses

Makes
2 servings

Ingredients

**1 cup = ? milliliters low-
fat or skim milk**

1 cup vanilla (or other flavor)
frozen yogurt or ice milk

1 tablespoon vanilla or
chocolate syrup

Steps

1. Pour the milk, syrup, and ice milk or frozen yogurt into
the blender container.

2. Cover and blend on medium speed until smooth.

3. Pour into glasses and serve.

CHAPTER 2

HOW MANY QUARTS IS A LITER OF MILK?

500 milliliters
= 1.06 pints

4 liters
= 1.06 gallons

Now that you've mastered converting measurements from English to metric units, let's try it the other way around. It should be easy to remember that a liter of milk is equal to 1.06 quarts, which is just about a quart. And that 4 liters equals 1.06 gallons, which is about a gallon, and that 500 milliliters equals 1.06 pints, or about a pint. A kilogram of steak equals 2.2 pounds, and 500 grams of sugar equals 1.1 pounds, which is about a pound.

The charts on the following page show how typical metric measurements compare to English measurements. Use the charts to practice converting measurements from metric to English units in the Math Activity.

1 liter
= 1.06 quarts

1 kilogram = 2.2 pounds

500 grams = 1.1 pounds

250 grams = 8.8 ounces

100 grams = 3.5 ounces

Volume

Metric	English
4 liters (l)	1.06 gallons (gal)
1 liter	1.06 quarts (qt)
500 milliliters (ml)	1.06 pints (pt)
240 milliliters	1 cup (c)
15 milliliters	1 tablespoon (Tbsp)
5 milliliters	1 teaspoon (tsp)

Weight

Metric	English
1 kilogram (kg)	2.2 pounds (lb)
500 grams (g)	1.1 pounds
340 grams	12 ounces (oz)
250 grams	8.8 ounces
100 grams	3.5 ounces
30 grams	1.1 ounces
28 grams	1 ounce

Length

Metric	English
1 meter (m)	1.1 yards (yd)
1 meter	3.3 feet (ft)
1 centimeter (cm)	.4 inches (in.)
1 millimeters (mm)	.04 inches

ENGLISH EXCHANGE

MATH ACTIVITY

Materials

3 charts above

pencil

notebook

Procedure

1. Change each of the following measurements of length from metric to English units.

   a. 1 meter = ? feet red licorice

   b. 2 centimeters = ? inches cracker

   c. 10 millimeter = ? inches raisin

2. Change each of the following measurements of volume from metric to English units.

  a. 4 liters = ? gallons apple cider

  b. 2 liters = ? quarts soda

  c. 500 milliliters = ? pints milk

3. Change each of the following measurements of weight from metric to English units.

  a. 1 kilogram = ? pounds green beans

  b. 500 grams = ? pounds hamburger meat

  c. 100 grams = ? ounces canned corn

Check your answers in Appendix A.

BISCUIT AND SCONE RECIPES

In each of these recipes, one of the measurements is shown in **boldface** type. That measurement is given in metric units. In the metric system, dry ingredients are measured by weight, not by volume as in the English system. Convert those measurements from metric to English units and check your answers in Appendix A when you're through.

Nutmeg Baking Powder Biscuits

Serve these biscuits warm with apple butter, jelly, or jam.

Ingredients

vegetable oil cooking spray

340 grams = ? ounces (2 cups) all-purpose flour

1 tablespoon baking powder

½ teaspoon baking soda

¼ teaspoon salt

¼ cup (½ stick) margarine, chilled

¾ cup low-fat buttermilk

1 tablespoon sugar

½ teaspoon nutmeg

extra flour for kneading

Steps

1. Preheat the oven to 400°F.

2. Spray the cookie sheet with vegetable oil cooking spray.

3. In the medium bowl, combine the flour, baking powder, baking soda, and salt. Mix well with the wooden spoon.

4. On the cutting board, use a table knife to cut the margarine into four pieces, then cut each piece in half. Place the margarine in the bowl with the flour mixture.

5. Use the pastry blender to cut through the margarine and dry ingredients. Keep cutting, using a back-and-forth rocking

Time
25 minutes to prepare
plus
10 to 12 minutes to bake

Tools
cookie sheet

medium bowl

wooden spoon

cutting board

pastry blender or 2 table knives

2-inch round biscuit cutter or small glass

small bowl

spoon

oven mitts

Makes
12 biscuits

• • • • •

If you don't have a pastry blender, use 2 table knives. Holding a knife in each hand, draw the knives across each other to cut through the margarine and dry ingredients. Keep cutting until the pieces of flour and margarine mixture are the size of small peas.

• • • • •

motion, until the pieces of the flour-and-margarine mixture are the size of small peas.

6. Stir in the buttermilk just until the dry ingredients are moistened.

• • • • •
Don't overknead the dough. Overkneading will make the biscuits tough.
• • • • •

7. Lightly sprinkle about 1 tablespoon of flour over the surface of the cutting board and place the dough on it. **Knead** the dough by pressing it out, then folding it in half. Give the dough a quarter turn after each fold and start again. Knead the dough for about 5 minutes or until the dough is satiny and smooth.

8. Pat the dough out to a thickness of ½ inch. Cut out the biscuits with the biscuit cutter or the rim of a small glass.

9. Mix together the sugar and the nutmeg in the small bowl. Use the spoon to lightly sprinkle the sugar mixture onto the biscuits.

10. Place the biscuits 1 inch apart on the sprayed cookie sheet.

11. Bake the biscuits for 10 to 12 minutes or until golden brown. Use oven mitts to remove the sheet from the oven. Let the biscuits cool for a few minutes before serving.

Say "Cheese Please" Scones

Scones are like biscuits, but they have a richer flavor because the dough contains eggs, cream, or butter.

Ingredients

vegetable oil cooking spray

2½ cups all-purpose flour

1 cup shredded sharp cheddar cheese

2 teaspoons dried basil

1 teaspoon dried chives

1 tablespoon baking powder

½ teaspoon salt

¾ cup (1½ sticks) chilled margarine or butter

2 eggs

120 ml = ? cups 2% milk

extra flour for kneading

Time
25 minutes to prepare
plus
15 minutes to bake

Tools
2 cookie sheets

large bowl

wooden spoon

cutting board

table knife

pastry blender

medium bowl

wire whip

3- or 4-inch round biscuit cutters

oven mitts

Makes
16 to 18 3-inch scones or
12 4-inch scones

Steps

1. Preheat the oven to 400°F.

2. Spray both cookie sheets with vegetable oil cooking spray.

3. Combine the flour, shredded cheese, basil, chives, baking powder, and salt together in the bowl. Mix well with the wooden spoon.

4. On the cutting board, use the table knife to cut the cold margarine into six pieces. Cut each piece in half again. Put the margarine into the flour mixture in the large bowl.

5. With the pastry blender, cut through the margarine and dry ingredients. Keep cutting the flour and margarine mixture until the pieces are the size of small peas. Set aside.

6. In the medium bowl, whisk together the eggs and the milk until foamy. Pour the egg mixture into the flour and margarine mixture and stir just until well blended to form a dough.

7. Lightly sprinkle about 2 tablespoons of flour over the surface of the cutting board and place the dough on it. Knead the dough by pressing it out, then folding it in half. Give the dough a quarter turn after each fold and start over. Repeat this process about 10 times or until the dough is smooth and silky.

8. Pat the dough out to a thickness of ½ inch. Cut each scone with the biscuit cutter.

9. Place scones 2 inches apart on the cookie sheets.

10. Bake for 12 to 15 minutes or until lightly browned on top. Use oven mitts to remove the cookie sheets from the oven. Let the scones cool a few minutes before serving.

Scones are often made with dried fruit, raisins, currants, or nuts. For a change of pace, add some chocolate chips.

Ingredients

vegetable oil cooking spray

2½ cups all-purpose flour

1 tablespoon baking powder

½ teaspoon salt

¾ cup (1½ sticks) chilled margarine

2 eggs

120 ml = ? cups 2% milk

½ cup chocolate minichips

½ cup raisins

extra flour for kneading

Steps

1. Preheat the oven to 400°F.

2. Spray both cookie sheets with vegetable oil cooking spray.

3. Combine the flour, baking powder, and salt together in the large bowl. Mix well with the wooden spoon.

4. On a cutting board, use the table knife to cut the cold margarine into six pieces. Cut each piece in half again. Put the margarine into the large bowl with the flour mixture.

5. Use the pastry blender to cut through the margarine and dry ingredients. Keep cutting the flour and margarine mixture until the pieces are the size of small peas. Set aside.

6. In the medium bowl, whisk together the eggs and the milk until foamy. Pour the egg mixture into the flour and margarine mixture, and stir just until well blended to form a dough.

7. Fold the chocolate chips and raisins into the dough.

Time

25 minutes to prepare plus
15 minutes to bake

Tools

2 cookie sheets

large bowl

wooden spoon

cutting board

table knife

pastry blender

medium bowl

wire whip

4-inch round biscuit cutter

Makes

12 4-inch scones

HOW MANY QUARTS IS A LITER OF MILK? ● ● ● 33

8. Lightly sprinkle about 2 tablespoons of flour over the surface of the cutting board and place the dough on it. Knead the dough by pressing it out, then folding it in half. Give the dough a quarter turn after each fold and start over. Repeat this process about 10 times or until the dough is smooth and silky.

9. Pat the dough out to a thickness of ½ inch. Cut each scone with the round biscuit cutter.

10. Place scones 2 inches apart on the cookie sheets.

11. Bake for 12 to 15 minutes or until lightly browned on top. Use oven mitts to remove the cookie sheets from the oven. Let the scones cool a few minutes before serving.

CHAPTER 3

HOW LONG IS THAT GIANT COOKIE?

If you're making a giant cookie that is 6 inches long at its widest part, you're measuring length. In the English system, units for length are inches, feet, yards, and miles.

English Units of Length	
1 foot (ft)	= 12 inches (in.)
1 yard (yd)	= 36 inches (in.)
1 yard	= 3 feet
1 mile (mi)	= 1,760 yards

In the metric system, the basic unit for length is the meter. The meter is a little longer than 1 yard (3 feet). One thousand meters equals 1 kilometer, which is a little more than half of a mile.

When you use a metric ruler, the numbers you see are centimeters, the markings between the numbers are millimeters. One centimeter equals 10 millimeters. A centimeter is a little less than ½ inch, and a millimeter is about the size of the thickness of a dime.

Metric Units of Length	
1 centimeter (cm)	= 10 millimeters (mm)
1 meter (m)	= 100 centimeters
1 kilometer (km)	= 1000 meters

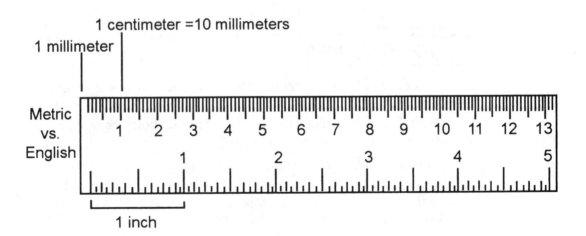

MATH ACTIVITY — RULER RAMPAGE

Materials

ruler with metric and English scales
1 piece of spaghetti or any pasta shape
1 slice of bread
1 slice of cheese
pencil
notebook

Procedure

1. Use your ruler to measure in inches and centimeters the length of the spaghetti or other pasta. Write your answers in your notebook.

2. Use your ruler to measure in inches and centimeters the height of a piece of bread. Write your answers in your notebook.

3. Use your ruler to measure in inches and centimeters the length of one side of the cheese slice. Write your answers in your notebook.

COOKIE RECIPES

For each of the following five cookie recipes, you'll need to use a ruler to measure the cookie dough balls. Measure across the widest part of the ball, called its **diameter**, which is shown in **boldface** type. You'll learn more about diameter later in this book.

The second **boldface** measurement in each recipe tells you how far apart to place the dough balls on the cookie sheet. Use the ruler to measure these lengths. After a while, you should be able to estimate, or guess, where to put the dough balls without using a ruler.

Giant Oatmeal Raisin Chocolate Chip Cookies

If you like big cookies, or you like oatmeal or raisins or chocolate chips (or all three), this is the cookie for you!

Ingredients

vegetable oil cooking spray

1½ cups (3 sticks) margarine, softened

1¾ cups brown sugar

2 eggs

2 tablespoons honey

1 tablespoon vanilla extract

1 teaspoon salt

2 cups all-purpose flour

2 pounds rolled oats

1 cup raisins

1 cup chocolate chips

1 cup chopped pecans or other nuts or chips

Steps

1. Preheat the oven to 350°F.

2. Spray the cookie sheets with vegetable oil cooking spray.

3. Put the margarine and brown sugar in the large bowl. Press the margarine and brown sugar against the bowl with the back of the wooden spoon until they are mixed together and look creamy.

4. Beat in the eggs, honey, vanilla extract, and salt. Mix thoroughly until the mixture is creamy.

5. Mix in the flour and oats.

6. Add the raisins, chocolate chips, and pecans and mix thoroughly.

7. Roll the dough into large **2-inch (50-millimeter)** balls.

8. Place 10 balls on each cookie sheet. Leave at least 2½ inches (60 millimeters) of space between each ball.

Time
20 minutes to prepare plus
30 minutes to bake in 2 batches

Tools
2 cookie sheets

large bowl

wooden spoon

spatula

oven mitts

cooling rack

Makes
About 36 large cookies

• • • • •

Honey is hard to measure because it sticks to the measuring tool. To prevent this, spray your tablespoon with vegetable oil cooking spray before measuring the honey.

• • • • •

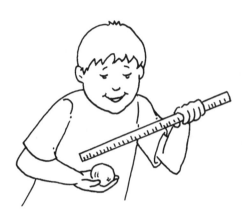

9. Press each ball down with the spatula to make flat cookies.

10. Bake the cookies for 15 minutes or until lightly golden brown on the bottom.

11. Remove the cookie sheets from the oven using oven mitts. Let the cookies cool for 10 minutes, then use the spatula to move them from the cookie sheets to the cooling rack. Store the cookies in an airtight container once cooled.

12. Wash, dry, and respray the cookie sheets with vegetable oil cooking spray.

13. Repeat steps 8 to 11 to make a second batch. If you have enough dough for a third batch, remember to wash, dry, and respray the cookie sheet before using it again.

Speckled Peanut Butter Chewies

These cookies are speckled with oatmeal and candy-coated chocolate bits. Eat them as a snack or pack them with your lunch.

Ingredients

½ cup peanut butter

⅓ cup (5⅓ tablespoons) margarine

½ cup brown sugar

1 egg

1 teaspoon vanilla extract

½ cup rolled oats

1 cup all-purpose flour

½ cup whole wheat flour

2 teaspoons baking powder

1 cup M&M's Mini-Baking Bits

colored sugar (optional)

Steps

1. Preheat the oven to 350°F.

2. Put the peanut butter, margarine, and brown sugar together in the bowl. Press the ingredients against the bowl with the back of the wooden spoon until they are mixed together and look creamy.

3. Add the egg and vanilla extract to the peanut butter mixture and stir well.

4. Add the rolled oats to the mixture and mix thoroughly.

5. Mix in the all-purpose flour, whole wheat flour, baking powder, and M&M's Mini-Baking Bits.

6. Roll the dough into **1-inch (25-millimeter)** balls.

7. Place cookie dough balls **2 inches (50 millimeters)** apart on ungreased cookie sheets. Use the fork to flatten and make a crisscross design on each cookie.

Time
20 minutes to prepare
plus
24 minutes to bake in 2 batches

Tools
medium bowl

wooden spoon

2 cookie sheets

fork

oven mitts

spatula

cooling rack

Makes
about 3 dozen cookies

• • • • •
You can put some colored sugar on the cookies just before baking for a colorful treat.
• • • • •

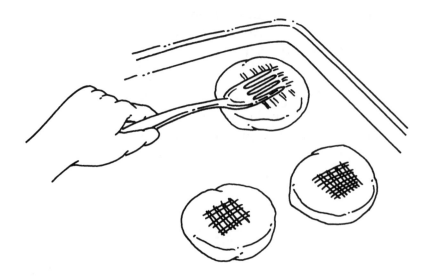

8. Bake the cookies for 10 to 12 minutes or until lightly golden brown.

9. Remove the cookie sheets from the oven using oven mitts. Let the cookies cool for 5 minutes, then use the spatula to move them from the cookie sheets to the cooling rack.

10. Wash and dry the cookie sheets.

11. Repeat steps 7 to 9 to make a second batch.

Lemon Drop Sugar Cookies

This recipe uses colored sugar to make beautiful multicolored treats.

Ingredients

1 cup (2 sticks) margarine, softened

1 cup sugar

1 egg

1 teaspoon lemon extract

2¼ cups all-purpose flour

1 teaspoon baking powder

colored sugar or table sugar for dipping

Steps

1. Preheat the oven to 350°F.

2. Put the margarine and sugar in the bowl. Press the margarine and sugar against the bowl with the back of the wooden spoon until they are mixed together and look creamy.

3. Add the egg and lemon extract.

4. Slowly mix in the flour and baking powder, then beat the mixture vigorously until it looks creamy and well combined.

5. Shape the dough into **1-inch (25-millimeter)** balls with your hands.

6. Place 10 cookie dough balls **2 inches (50 millimeters)** apart on each ungreased cookie sheet.

7. Put about ¼ cup colored sugar on the plates. Hold the bottom of the drinking glass under running water to wet it. Then dip the bottom of the glass in the colored sugar. Use the sugar-covered glass to flatten the cookies.

8. Bake the cookies for 12 to 15 minutes or until lightly golden brown.

Time
30 minutes to prepare
plus
30 minutes to bake
2 batches

Tools
2 cookie sheets

medium bowl

wooden spoon

plate

drinking glass with flat bottom

oven mitts

spatula

cooling rack

Makes
3 dozen cookies

9. Remove the cookie sheets from the oven using oven mitts. Let the cookies cool for 5 minutes, then use the spatula to move them from the cookie sheets to a cooling rack.

10. Wash and dry the cookie sheets.

11. Repeat steps 7 to 9 to make a second batch.

Awesome Animal Crackers

Use your favorite animal cookie cutters to make these fun crackers.

Ingredients

1 cup rolled oats

¼ cup honey

1 teaspoon salt

1½ cups all-purpose flour

½ teaspoon baking soda

½ teaspoon cinnamon

½ cup (1 stick) cold butter

½ cup buttermilk

2 tablespoons extra all-purpose flour

Steps

1. Preheat the oven to 400°F.

2. Put the rolled oats in the blender container. Cover and blend at high speed to grind the rolled oats into oat flour. (The oat flour will look powdery.)

3. Place the oat flour in the bowl. Add the honey, salt, all-purpose flour, baking soda, and cinnamon to the bowl and stir well with the wooden spoon.

4. Take the butter out of the refrigerator and cut it into 8 equal pieces. Place the butter in the flour mixture.

5. With the pastry blender, cut the butter into the dry ingredients by using a back-and-forth rocking motion until the bits of butter-flour mixture are the size of small peas.

6. Add the buttermilk to the bowl and mix thoroughly with your hands until the mixture forms a dough. Continue to mix together until smooth.

7. Allow the dough to sit for 5 minutes.

8. Sprinkle the extra 2 tablespoons of flour over a clean surface.

Time
20 minutes to prepare
plus
10 to 12 minutes to bake

Tools
blender

large bowl

wooden spoon

table knife

pastry blender or 2 table knives

rolling pin

animal cookie cutters

cookie sheet

spatula

oven mitts

cooling rack

Makes
12 to 24 crackers

• • • • •

You can use any other shape cookie cutters for this recipe if you wish.

• • • • •

9. With the rolling pin, roll out the dough until it is ¼-inch **(6 millimeters)** thick.

10. Cut the dough with animal cookie cutters.

11. Use the spatula to place the crackers **2 inches (50 millimeters)** apart on the ungreased cookie sheet.

12. Bake the crackers for 10 to 12 minutes or until lightly golden brown.

13. Remove the cookie sheets from the oven using oven mitts. Let the crackers cool for 5 minutes, then use the spatula to move them from the cookie sheets to the cooling rack.

Taste-of-Honey Spread

Try this quick and sweet spread on Awesome Animal Crackers and on biscuits, too.

Time
15 minutes

Tools
medium bowl

electric mixer

Makes
24 1-tablespoon servings

Ingredients

½ cup honey

1 cup (2 sticks) margarine, softened

1 tablespoon confectioners' sugar

Steps

1. Put the honey, margarine, and sugar in the bowl. Use the electric mixer on medium speed to beat the mixture until it is light and fluffy, about 3 to 5 minutes.

2. Spread the honey mixture on cooled Awesome Animal Crackers.

•••• Microwave Chocolate •••• Walnut Cookies

Time
20 to 25 minutes to prepare
plus
up to 8 minutes to microwave

Tools
large bowl

wooden spoon

medium bowl

5 paper plates

spoon

spatula

oven mitts

cooling rack

Makes
30 cookies

It's not always easy to make a good cookie in the microwave, but this recipe works very well. Once you make the cookie dough, you can keep it in the refrigerator for 2 to 3 days and micro-wave cookies in batches when you want them.

Ingredients

¾ cup margarine (1½ sticks), left at room temperature for 1 hour

¾ cup sugar

1 egg

1¾ cups flour

¼ cup unsweetened cocoa powder

1 teaspoon baking powder

½ teaspoon salt

1 teaspoon vanilla extract

½ cup chopped walnuts

½ cup sugar

Steps

1. Put the margarine and ¾ cup sugar in the large bowl. Use the wooden spoon to cream them together until smooth and light. Add the egg and mix thoroughly.

2. Put the flour, cocoa powder, baking powder, and salt in the medium bowl. Blend ingredients well.

3. Add the flour mixture to the margarine bowl. Stir just until blended.

4. Add the vanilla extract and walnuts. Stir well.

5. With your hands, pinch off pieces of dough and roll into **1-inch (25-millimeter)** balls.

6. Put ½ cup sugar on a paper plate. Roll the balls of dough in the sugar, one at a time, and then place them about **1½ inches (35 millimeters)** apart on the other paper plates. Put 7 to 8 cookies on a plate. Lightly flatten the tops of the cookies with the back of the spoon.

7. Microwave one plate of cookies at a time on full power (high) until they are puffed up. This will take about 2 minutes for 8 cookies. Use oven mitts to remove the paper plates from the microwave.

8. Let the cookies cool for a minute before using the spatula to put them on the cooling rack. The cookies will become firmer as they cool.

CHAPTER 4

HOW MUCH SOUP IS IN A BOWL OF SOUP?

Soup—and all liquids—can be measured by volume, which is a measurement of how much space something takes up. In the English system there are many units to measure volume. There are teaspoons, tablespoons, fluid ounces, cups, pints, quarts, and gallons.

1 teaspoon   1 tablepoon   1 cup

1 pint   1 quart

1 half gallon   1 gallon

In the metric system, there are only two ways to measure volume: in milliliters and liters. One liter contains 1000 milliliters (*milli-* means thousand).

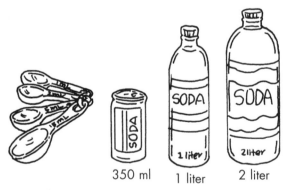

350 ml   1 liter   2 liter

Try the following math activity to learn more about volume.

VA, VA, VA . . . VOLUME!

Materials:

tablespoon

teaspoon

1-cup (250-milliliter) and 2-cup (500-milliliter) measuring cups
  with spouts

1-quart and 1-gallon measuring containers (You can use a clean,
  empty gallon milk jug.)

1-liter measuring container (You can use a clean, empty soda
  bottle.)

pencil

notebook

Procedure

Using your measuring devices and water, see how
many teaspoons are needed to fill 1 tablespoon, how many
tablespoons of water are needed to fill 1 cup, how many
cups of water are needed to fill 1 pint, and so on as follows. Record your answers as a chart in your notebook.

a. 1 tablespoon = ? teaspoons

b. 1 cup = ? tablespoons

c. 1 pint = ? cups

d. 1 quart = ? cups

e. 1 quart = ? pints

f. 1 gallon = ? quarts

g. 1 liter = ? milliliters

h. 1 tablespoon = ? fluid ounces

i. 1 cup = ? fluid ounces

j. 1 pint = ? fluid ounces

k. 1 quart = ? fluid ounces

l. 1 gallon = ? fluid ounces

Check your answers in Appendix A.

SOUP RECIPES

In each of these recipes, you'll need to use your chart from the Math
Activity to write the measurement in another way for the ingredients
shown in **boldface** type. Check your answers in Appendix A.

···· Rib-Stickin' Chicken ····
and Number Soup

Time
20 minutes to prepare
plus
60 minutes to cook

Tools
serrated knife

cutting board

plate

clear plastic wrap

paring knife

vegetable peeler

stockpot

wooden spoon

can opener

Makes
8 1½-cup servings

• • • • •

*Some raw chicken
contains germs that can
make you sick. Make sure
you wash the knife and
cutting board thoroughly
with hot water and soap,
then rinse carefully.*

• • • • •

*Number or alphabet soup macaroni
makes this soup really fun to eat!*

Ingredients

1½ pounds chicken cutlets

3 stalks celery

2 carrots

2 medium onions

¼ cup olive oil

**4 cups = ? quarts
canned chicken broth**

4 cups water

1 15-ounce can whole-kernel corn

1 cup frozen cut green beans, thawed

1 teaspoon minced fresh chives

1 tablespoon Worcestershire sauce

1 teaspoon salt

¼ teaspoon pepper

1 cup number or alphabet soup macaroni

Steps

1. Using the serrated knife on the cutting board, cut the chicken into ½-inch cubes. Place on a plate, cover with plastic wrap, and refrigerate until step 13.

2. Wash the knife and cutting board thoroughly.

3. Wash and pat dry the celery and carrots.

4. On the clean cutting board, use the paring knife to slice the celery lengthwise into two strips, then cut them into small pieces.

5. Peel the carrots with the vegetable peeler. Use the paring knife to slice the peeled carrots into ¼-inch slices.

6. Remove the outer skin from the onions.

7. Cut each onion in half on the cutting board. Lay each onion half flat and cut into ¼-inch slices.

8. Preheat the stockpot by placing it on a burner and setting the heat to medium for 2 minutes.

9. Put the oil in the stockpot.

10. Add the celery, carrot, and onion pieces to the stockpot. Sauté about 5 minutes until tender, stirring with the wooden spoon.

11. Add chicken broth and water to the pot. Simmer uncovered for 15 minutes.

12. Open the can of corn and drain the liquid.

13. Add the chicken cubes, corn, and green beans to the pot. Stir well.

14. Add the chives, Worcestershire sauce, salt, and pepper to the pot. Cover the soup and simmer for 30 minutes.

15. Add the number or alphabet macaroni. Cook the soup, uncovered, for an additional 15 minutes, stirring the soup occasionally so the macaroni does not stick to the pot.

Zippy Vegetable Soup with Mini-Bow-Tie Pasta

Time
30 minutes to prepare plus
1 hour to cook

Tools
cutting board

paring knife

vegetable peeler

stockpot with lid

wooden spoon

can opener

Makes
8 1½ cup servings

• • • • •
Scallions, also called green onions, are onions that are immature, or not fully grown.
• • • • •

When you serve this soup, ask if people can guess how many different vegetables it contains. (Did they miss the scallions?)

Ingredients

5 scallions

3 carrots

4 celery stalks

2 cups button mushrooms

2 red potatoes

¼ cup olive oil

1 15-ounce can red kidney beans

1 28-ounce can crushed tomatoes

1 tablespoon dried thyme

1 tablespoon dried oregano

1½ cups frozen cut green beans, thawed

8 cups vegetable broth, canned or homemade

½ liter = ? milliliters (2 cups) water

1½ cups (360 ml) mini-bow-tie pasta

Steps

1. Wash and dry the scallions, carrots, celery, and mushrooms.

2. On the cutting board, use the paring knife to cut the root end and the green stems off the scallions. Cut the white part of the scallions into ¼-inch pieces.

3. Peel the carrots with the vegetable peeler, then cut the peeled carrots into ¼-inch slices.

4. Cut the ends off of the celery stalks. Slice each lengthwise into 2 strips, then cut them into small pieces.

5. Slice the mushrooms into ¼-inch slices.

6. Wash and dry the potatoes. Use the vegetable peeler to peel the outer skin off the potatoes.

7. Slice each potato into ¼-inch slices. Cut each slice into small cubes.

8. Preheat the stockpot by placing it on a burner and setting the heat to medium for 2 minutes.

9. Put the oil in the stockpot.

10. Add the scallions, carrots, and celery to the stockpot. Sauté about 5 minutes until tender, stirring with the wooden spoon.

11. Open the cans of kidney beans and crushed tomatoes. Place the kidney beans (including the liquid they are in), potatoes, crushed tomatoes, thyme, and oregano in the pot.

12. Cover the pot and simmer for 15 minutes.

13. Add green beans, mushroom slices, vegetable broth, and water. Stir well.

14. Cover again and simmer for 30 minutes.

15. Add the bow-tie pasta. Cook the soup for an additional 15 minutes, uncovered. Stir the soup occasionally so the pasta won't stick to the pot.

Corn-off-the-Cob Chowder

Time
25 minutes to prepare plus
65 minutes to cook

Tools
2 paper towels

microwave-safe plate

oven mitts

cutting board

paring knife

stockpot

vegetable brush

vegetable peeler

wooden spoon

can opener

Makes
6 1½-cup servings

If you like corn-on-the-cob, you'll love this soup!

Ingredients

6 strips of bacon

2 medium onions

3 celery stalks

2 tablespoons butter

6 small red potatoes

1 cup = ? fluid ounces water

2 cups chicken stock

4 15-ounce cans whole-kernel corn

1 teaspoon salt

¼ teaspoon pepper

1 tablespoon dried chopped chives

4 cups 2% milk

Steps

1. Lay 1 paper towel on the microwave-safe plate. Place the strips of bacon on the paper towel and cover with the second paper towel.

2. Put the plate in the microwave and cook on high for 4 to 5 minutes, until the bacon is crisp. Use oven mitts to remove plate and set aside.

3. Remove the papery skin from the onions.

4. On the cutting board, use the paring knife to cut the onions in half. Lay each half flat and cut into ¼-inch slices.

5. Wash and dry the celery stalks. Cut the ends off of the celery stalks, slice the stalks lengthwise into 2 long pieces, then cut them into small pieces.

6. Preheat the stockpot by placing it on a burner and setting the heat to medium for 2 minutes.

7. Put the butter in the stockpot.

8. When the butter has melted, add the onions and celery. Stirring with the wooden spoon, sauté them until golden and tender, about 5 minutes. Turn the heat to low.

9. Scrub the potatoes with the vegetable brush under running water. Use the vegetable peeler to peel the outer skin off the potatoes.

10. Slice each potato into ¼-inch slices and cut each slice into small cubes.

11. Add the potato cubes to the stockpot. Stir well.

12. Add the water and chicken broth to the stockpot. Stir.

13. Carefully open each can of corn. Add the corn and its liquid to the stockpot.

14. Season the soup with the salt, pepper, and chives.

15. Cover the pot and simmer the soup for 45 minutes, or until the potatoes are tender.

16. Add the milk. Simmer the soup, uncovered, for an additional 20 minutes.

Mexican Jumpin' Bean Soup

Time
20 minutes to prepare
plus
30 minutes to cook

Tools
2 paper towels

microwave-safe plate

oven mitts

cutting board

paring knife

stockpot

wooden spoon

can opener

Makes
6 1½-cup servings

*Serve this soup with shredded cheese
on top and nacho chips!*

Ingredients

6 strips of bacon

2 medium onions

2 celery stalks

2 tablespoons margarine

2 cups = ? pint water

2 15-ounce cans pinto beans

1 15-ounce can red kidney beans

1 tablespoon dried cilantro

¾ cup medium salsa

2 cups shredded Monterey Jack cheese

1 bag of nacho chips

Steps

1. Lay 1 paper towel on the microwave-safe plate. Place the strips of bacon on the paper towel and cover with the second paper towel.

2. Put the plate in the microwave and cook on high for 4 to 5 minutes, until the bacon is crisp. Use oven mitts to remove plate and set aside.

3. Remove the papery skin from the onions.

4. On a cutting board, use the paring knife to cut the onions in half. Lay each half flat and cut it into ¼-inch slices.

5. Wash and dry the celery stalks. Cut the ends off of the celery stalks. Slice the stalks lengthwise into 2 long pieces, then cut them into small pieces.

6. Preheat the stockpot by placing it on a burner and setting the heat to medium for 2 minutes.

7. Put the margarine in the stockpot.

8. When the margarine has melted, add the onions and celery. Stirring with the wooden spoon, sauté them until golden and tender, about 5 minutes.

9. Crumble the bacon and add it to the stockpot.

10. Add the water and stir well.

11. Open the cans of pinto beans and kidney beans and drain the liquid from the beans. Add the beans, cilantro, and salsa to the pot and stir well.

12. Bring the mixture to a boil over a high heat.

13. Lower the heat until the soup is simmering. Cover the pot and cook for about 30 minutes.

14. Ladle the soup into bowls and sprinkle with Monterey Jack cheese. Serve with nacho chips.

●●●●●
Beans are one of the best sources of fiber. Fiber is a type of carbohydrate that is present in healthy foods such as fruits, vegetables, and grains.
●●●●●

···· Melon Soup ····

Time
20 minutes

Tools
knife

cutting board

spoon

melon baller (optional)

electric blender

can opener

soup bowls

Makes
6 1-cup servings

Soups don't always have to be hot. Fruits, such as melons, and vegetables, such as tomatoes, are often used to make cold soups. This cold soup is great on a hot summer day.

Ingredients

1 small cantaloupe

1 20-ounce can crushed pineapple, packed in its own juice

1 cup crushed ice

1 cup = ? pint pineapple juice

½ cup plain low-fat yogurt

Steps

1. Wash and dry the cantaloupe. Use the knife to cut the cantaloupe in half on the cutting board.

2. Remove the seeds from the cantaloupe halves with the spoon and discard the seeds.

3. Use the spoon or a melon baller to scoop out as many melon balls as possible from one of the cantaloupe halves and put the melon balls in the container of the electric blender.

4. Open the can of crushed pineapple and add the pineapple with its juice to the blender.

5. Add the crushed ice. Put the lid on the blender. Blend at high speed until the mixture is smooth.

6. Scoop out the second cantaloupe half and add the melon balls to the blender. Blend until smooth.

7. Add enough pineapple juice to the cantaloupe to make it just thick enough for soup.

8. Pour into bowls. Place a heaping tablespoon of yogurt on top of each one and serve.

CHAPTER 5

WHAT DOES A HANDFUL OF PASTA WEIGH?

Pasta and other solids can be measured by weight. Using the English system, the weight of an object is measured in ounces (oz), pounds (lb), and even tons (T) if it's really heavy. For example, two tablespoons of sugar weigh about 1 ounce. A typical bag of sugar weighs 5 pounds, and a tanker truck carrying sugar to the soft drink plant weighs many tons. A ton is 2000 pounds!

2 tablespoons of sugar = 1 ounce

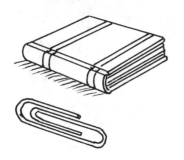

Using the metric system, the weight of an object is measured in milligrams (mg), centigrams (cg), grams (g), and kilograms (kg). There are 1000 milligrams and 100 centigrams in one gram. A large paper clip or half a LifeSavers candy each weigh about 1 gram. There are 1000 grams in a kilogram. A kilogram is just a little more than 2 pounds. A typical book weighs about 1 kilogram.

HOW HEAVY?

MATH ACTIVITY

Materials

table fork

salt shaker

measuring cup

peanut butter jar

loaf of bread

kitchen scale

pencil

notebook

Procedure

1. Order the first five materials by size, from smallest to largest.

2. Next, order the materials by weight, from what feels to be the lightest to what feels to be the heaviest.

3. Use the scale to weigh each item and record its weight. Rearrange the objects by their actual weight from lightest to heaviest. Which object is the lightest? Which object is the heaviest? Are smaller objects always lighter in weight than larger objects?

4. Answer the following questions and write the answers in your notebook.

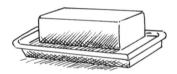

a. Does this turkey weigh about 14 oz or 14 lb?

b. A stick of margarine weighs about 4 lb or 4 oz?

c. A baby weighs 4 kilograms or 40 kilograms?

Check your answers in Appendix A.

PASTA AND PASTA SAUCE RECIPES

Each of the following recipes has an ingredient in **boldface** type. Those ingredients have to be weighed. Use a kitchen scale to weigh them, using either English or metric units.

····Fantastic Fettuccini····

Fettuccini is a flat, narrow pasta that looks like ribbon. Some fettuccini is green—it contains spinach.

Ingredients

3 quarts water

1 teaspoon salt

½ pound (225 grams) fettuccini noodles

¼ cup (½ stick) butter

½ cup light cream

½ cup 1% or 2% milk

½ teaspoon salt

¼ teaspoon pepper

½ cup grated Parmesan cheese

¼ teaspoon nutmeg

¼ cup dried chopped chives

Steps

1. Pour the water into the stockpot.

2. Bring the water to a rapid boil by placing the covered stockpot on the burner and turning the heat to high. It should take about 8 to 15 minutes for the water to boil.

3. Add the salt to the boiling water.

4. Slowly add the fettuccini to the pot and stir well with the long-handled fork.

5. Cook the fettuccini, uncovered, over high heat for 10 minutes or until the pasta is tender. Stir occasionally.

6. Put the colander in the sink. Use the oven mitts to lift the pot and carefully pour the contents into the colander.

7. Preheat a large skillet by placing it on a burner and setting the heat to medium for 2 minutes.

8. Put the butter in the skillet and stir it constantly with the wooden spoon until the butter melts.

Time
20 minutes to prepare
plus
15 minutes to cook

Tools
4-quart stockpot

long-handled fork

colander

oven mitts

large skillet

wooden spoon

large serving bowl

2 spoons

Makes
4 1-cup servings

9. Add the cream and milk to the skillet and continue to stir.

10. Mix in the salt and pepper. Simmer the cream mixture for about 2 minutes until it thickens slightly.

11. Place the cooked fettuccini in the large serving bowl.

12. Add the cream and milk sauce, Parmesan cheese, and nutmeg to the fettuccini. Gently toss with 2 spoons to coat the pasta with the sauce.

13. Sprinkle the chopped chives over the top of the pasta to garnish and serve immediately.

···· Zero Meat Tomato Sauce ····

With this recipe you can make your own tomato sauce to use on your favorite pasta.

Ingredients

2½ quarts water

2 pounds (900 grams) tomatoes

1 medium onion

¼ cup olive oil

½ teaspoon sugar

1 teaspoon dried basil leaves

1 teaspoon dried oregano

1 teaspoon garlic powder

½ teaspoon salt

Steps

1. Fill the saucepan with the water and heat to a full boil.

2. Wash the tomatoes and pat dry.

3. On the cutting board, use the paring knife to cut an "X" at the top and bottom of each tomato.

4. Using the slotted spoon, carefully place the tomatoes in the boiling water and leave them there for 3 to 4 minutes. Do not let the water splash you.

5. Remove the tomatoes with the slotted spoon and put them in the colander. Rinse the tomatoes in cold water.

6. Peel the skins off the tomatoes with your hands or the paring knife. Scoop out the seeds of the tomato with the spoon.

7. On the cutting board, use the paring knife to chop the tomatoes into bite-size pieces.

8. Remove the papery skin from the onion.

9. On the cutting board, use the paring knife to cut the onion in half. Chop each half into bite-size pieces.

Time
20 minutes to prepare
plus
40 minutes to cook

Tools
4-quart saucepan

cutting board

paring knife

metal slotted spoon

large colander

spoon

stockpot

wooden spoon

Makes
10 to 12 ½-cup servings

• • • • •
Boiling then cooling the tomatoes makes their skins easy to remove.
• • • • •

10. Preheat a stockpot by placing it on a burner and setting the heat to medium for 2 minutes.

11. Put the olive oil in the pot.

12. Add the onions and sauté, stirring with the wooden spoon until they are golden brown and tender, about 5 minutes.

13. Add the tomatoes to the pot and stir well with the wooden spoon.

14. Add the sugar, basil, oregano, and garlic powder to the pot. Stir well. Cover the pot and simmer the sauce for 20 minutes.

15. Season with salt. Simmer, uncovered, for an additional 20 minutes.

······ ···· Garden Tomato and Basil Sauce ···· ······

This recipe uses fresh tomatoes and basil for flavor. Basil is an herb that tastes spicy and sweet.

Ingredients

1½ pounds (700 g) tomatoes

1 small onion

6 large fresh basil leaves

¼ cup olive oil

½ teaspoon garlic salt

½ cup grated Parmesan cheese

Steps

1. Wash the tomatoes and pat dry.

2. On the cutting board, use the paring knife to cut the tomatoes in half. Spoon out the seeds, then cut the tomatoes into bite-size pieces. Put them in a bowl and set aside.

3. Remove the outer skin of the onion. On the cutting board, use the paring knife to cut the onion in half, then chop the halves into small pieces.

4. Pull the basil leaves from their stems. Wash the leaves and lay them on a paper towel. Place the second paper towel over them and blot them dry.

5. Place the basil leaves on top of one another. Roll up the basil leaves lengthwise. Place the rolled basil leaves on the cutting board and cut crosswise into very thin circles. Lightly chop the cut basil.

6. Preheat a large frying pan by placing the pan on a burner and setting the heat to medium for 2 minutes.

7. Put the olive oil in the pan. Allow the oil to warm for about 2 minutes, or until it shimmers in the pan.

Time
20 to 25 minutes

Tools
cutting board

paring knife

spoon

small bowl

2 paper towels

large frying pan

wooden spoon

Makes
8 ½-cup servings

• • • • •
Don't substitute another kind of cooking oil. The taste of the olive oil makes the sauce special.
• • • • •

8. Add the tomatoes and basil to the olive oil.

9. Sprinkle the tomatoes with garlic salt and stir with the wooden spoon.

10. Simmer for 8 to 10 minutes to cook and blend the flavors. Be careful not to overcook because the sauce will become thick and mushy.

11. Serve the sauce over cooked pasta and sprinkle with Parmesan cheese.

Scooped Tomatoes Stuffed with Tuna Pasta Salad

If you cook the pasta for this recipe ahead of time, you can quickly make this dish without any further cooking. This is a great supper meal on a hot summer night.

Ingredients

½ pound (225 grams) tri-colored rotini pasta

6 large tomatoes

2 stalks celery

1 10½-ounce can tuna fish packed in water

½ cup low-fat mayonnaise dressing

½ teaspoon salt

6 sprigs of fresh parsley

Time
30 minutes

Tools
large saucepan with cover

wooden spoon

colander

oven mitts

large mixing bowl

cutting board

paring knife

spoon

paper towels

can opener

small bowl

Makes
6 tomatoes

Steps

1. Bring 2 to 3 quarts of water to a boil in the large, covered saucepan.

2. Add the pasta in 2 batches, stirring well with the wooden spoon after each addition. Cook the pasta for about 10 minutes or until tender.

3. Place the colander in the sink. When the pasta is done, use the oven mitts to lift the saucepan and pour the pasta into the colander. Rinse the pasta with cold water and let it drain well. Transfer the pasta to the large mixing bowl.

4. While the pasta is cooking, wash and dry the tomatoes and celery.

5. On the cutting board, use the paring knife to cut the top off each tomato.

6. Use the spoon to scoop out the center of the tomatoes. Turn the tomatoes upside down on paper towels to drain.

7. On the cutting board, use the paring knife to slice the celery into ¼-inch slices. Add to the large mixing bowl with the pasta.

8. Open the can of tuna fish and drain the liquid. Mix the tuna fish, mayonnaise, and salt in the small bowl.

9. Add the tuna fish mixture to the pasta. Stir to mix.

10. Scoop the pasta mixture into the tomatoes. Garnish with the parsley and serve.

CHAPTER 6
HOW DO YOU COOK CANDY?

All candy is made by cooking sugar mixtures at high temperatures. At different temperatures you get different types of candy. So to make candy, you need to know how to use a thermometer correctly. You read a thermometer by reading the mark on the number scale at the top of the glass tube.

There are two scales used to measure temperature, the **Fahrenheit** scale and the **Celsius** scale. On the Fahrenheit scale, the unit for measuring temperature is the degree Fahrenheit (°F). There are five divisions or lines between each printed number on the Fahrenheit scale. Each line equals two degrees. The Fahrenheit scale shown reads 78 degrees.

The metric unit for temperature is the degree Celsius (°C). On the Celsius scale, there are ten divisions or lines between each printed number. Each line equals one degree. The Celsius scale shown reads 32 degrees.

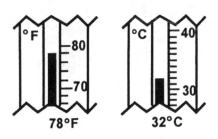

Now let's compare temperatures on the Fahrenheit and Celsius thermometers.

	Fahrenheit	Celsius
Water boils at	212°F	100°C
Water freezes at	32°F	0°C
A moderate oven is	350°F	175°C
Room temperature is about	70°F	20°C
A cold day might be	20°F	–10°C
A warm day might be	85°F	30°C

Try the Math Activity for practice reading temperatures using both the Fahrenheit and Celsius scales.

HOW HOT?

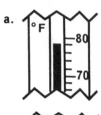

a.

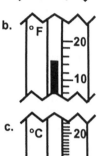

b.

c.

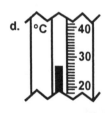

d.

Materials

4 thermometers shown
pencil
notebook

Procedures

1. Write down each temperature shown on the thermometers. The top two scales are Fahrenheit. The bottom two scales are Celsius.

2. Choose the food closest to the given temperature. Record your answers in your notebook.

a. 122°F, 50°C   cold water

warm soup

ice cube

b. 14°F, – 10°C   cold soda

slice of cheese

ice cream

Check your answers in Appendix A.

CANDY RECIPES

Each of the following recipes uses a special thermometer called a candy thermometer. Clip the candy thermometer to the side of the pan. Each recipe shows the temperature you should look for on the thermometer in **boldface** type. **The tip of the thermometer should be at least 1 inch in the liquid but should not touch the bottom of the pan.** Have fun!

*CAUTION: Be very careful when making candy because it requires high cooking temperatures. **Only** make candy with adult supervision, and be sure to keep small children and curious animals out of the kitchen.*

···· Caramel Candy Cubes ····

In candy-making, the higher the temperature, the harder the candy will be. For example, a caramel is cooked to 238°F (114°C) and a toffee is cooked to 280°F (138°C). The higher temperature for the toffee results in a harder candy than the caramel, which is chewy.

Time
35 minutes to cook
plus
4 hours to harden

Tools
9-inch square baking pan
3-quart saucepan
wooden spoon
candy thermometer
paring knife

Makes
64 ½-ounce pieces

Ingredients

vegetable oil cooking spray

1 cup (2 sticks) margarine

2¼ cups light brown sugar

¼ teaspoon salt

1 cup light corn syrup

1 14-ounce can sweetened condensed milk

1 teaspoon vanilla extract

Steps

1. Spray the baking pan with vegetable oil cooking spray. Set aside.

2. Preheat the saucepan by placing the pan on the burner and turning the heat to medium for 1 minute.

3. Put the margarine in the saucepan and stir with the wooden spoon until the margarine is melted.

4. Add the brown sugar and salt to the pan and stir until dissolved. Stir in the corn syrup.

5. In a slow, steady stream, carefully add the condensed milk to the pan, stirring constantly.

6. Attach a candy thermometer to the side of the pan.

7. Cook and stir steadily over medium heat until the thermometer reads **245°F (118°C)**, usually about 12 to 15 minutes. (This is called the **firm-ball** stage of candy making.)

• • • • •
Candies are made by boiling sugar and water until some of the water evaporates. If lots of water evaporates, the sugar syrup will make hard candy. If less water evaporates, the sugar syrup will make a softer candy such as a caramel.
• • • • •

8. Remove the caramel mixture from the heat and stir in the vanilla extract.

9. Carefully pour the mixture into the sprayed pan.

10. Allow the candy to thoroughly cool and harden. This usually takes about 4 hours.

11. Use a sharp paring knife to cut the candy into small cubes. Store the candy that is not eaten in an airtight container to maintain freshness.

···· Mallo-Mallo Fudge Squares ····

A box of this fudge would make a
great present for a special friend.

Ingredients

vegetable oil cooking spray

1 cup (2 sticks) margarine

4 cups sugar

12 fluid ounces evaporated
milk

1¾ cup semisweet chocolate
chips

1 10-ounce jar marshmallow
creme

1 cup chopped pecans

1 teaspoon vanilla extract

Steps

1. Spray the baking pan with vegetable oil cooking spray.
Set aside.

2. Preheat the saucepan by placing the pan on a burner
and turning the heat to medium for 1 minute.

3. Put the margarine in the saucepan. Stir with the
wooden spoon until the margarine is melted.

4. Add the sugar and stir until it dissolves.

5. Add the evaporated milk and stir until well blended.

6. Clip a candy thermometer on the side of the pan.
Cook the mixture, stirring constantly, until the thermometer reaches **236°F (113°C)**. (This is called the
soft-ball stage of candy making.)

7. Remove the pan from the heat and stir in the chocolate
chips, marshmallow creme, pecans, and vanilla extract
until well blended.

8. Pour the mixture into the sprayed pan and spread evenly
with the sandwich spreader or table knife.

9. Use the paring knife to score the fudge into squares as
if you were going to serve it. When you score fudge,
you make a shallow notch or cut into it. Let the fudge
cool in the pan at room temperature for about 3 hours.
Once cool, you can cut the fudge and remove it from
the pan.

Time
20 minutes to cook
plus
3 hours to cool

Tools
13- x 9-inch baking pan

3-quart saucepan

wooden spoon

candy thermometer

sandwich spreader or table
knife

paring knife

Makes
48 pieces

• • • • •

The soft-ball stage of
candy making got its
name because the sugar
syrup will make a soft
ball when rolled in your
fingers in ice water. Don't
try making a soft ball
yourself—this technique
is used by professional
cooks who are not using
a candy thermometer to
tell them when the syrup
needs no further cooking.

• • • • •

Brown Sugar Turtle Pralines

Time
30 to 40 minutes to make
plus
30 minutes to cool

Tools
cutting board

paring knife

2-quart saucepan

wooden spoon

candy thermometer

tablespoon

waxed paper

Makes
24 candies

A **praline** is a rich, patty-shaped candy made with sugar, cream, butter, and pecans. To make your pralines look like turtles, follow the directions.

Ingredients

2 cups pecan halves

2 cups light brown sugar

1 cup light cream

2 tablespoons butter

Steps

1. On the cutting board, use the paring knife to cut ½ cup of pecans halves into quarters by cutting each pecan horizontally into two pieces. Set aside.

2. Use the wooden spoon to combine the light brown sugar and the cream in the saucepan.

3. Bring the sugar and cream mixture to boil over a medium heat, stirring constantly.

4. Clip a candy thermometer to the side of the saucepan. Continue to cook the mixture until the thermometer reads **238°F (114°C)** (the soft-ball stage).

5. Remove the pan from the heat. Stir in the butter.

6. Stir in the remaining 1½ cups of pecan halves.

7. Beat the candy for 2 minutes or until it loses its shine.

8. Drop the candy by tablespoon onto waxed paper. Use the back of the spoon to shape the patties into a round shape.

9. Use the pecan quarters to decorate the candies to look like turtles. Put 2 pecan quarters at the front and 2 at the back for legs. Put 1 pecan quarter in between the front legs as the head.

10. Refrigerate the candy until cool, at least 30 minutes, before serving.

PART 2

ARITHMETIC

Is arithmetic important in the kitchen? Definitely! Do you want to double a recipe? Use multiplication. Are you cutting a recipe in half? Division does the job. Need to know how much lettuce you'll need for a salad for four? Try estimating. These arithmetic skills are some of the secret weapons of a great Math Chef!

CHAPTER 7

HOW DO YOU TRIPLE A SANDWICH RECIPE?

To find out how many total tomato slices you'll need to put two slices on each of three sandwiches, you can add the slices. To find the answer faster, you can multiply the number in each group (2) by the number of groups (3). The numbers that are multiplied are called **factors**, and the answer of the multiplication is called the **product**. For practice, let's multiply cookies that just came out of the oven.

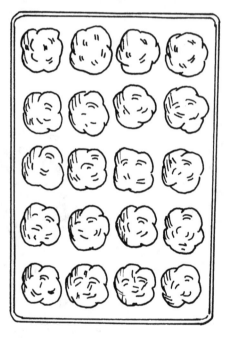

4 × 5 = 20

3 × 4 = 12

Turn to the Food Pyramid on p. 167. The Food Pyramid shows how many servings of the five food groups we need to eat every day. How many servings do you need from the Milk and Vegetable Groups each week? To answer that question, multiply each number by 7 as shown.

Daily Servings	Weekly Servings
Milk Group	
2 to 3 servings	14 (2 × 7) to 21 (3 × 7) servings
Vegetable Group	
3 to 5 servings	21 (3 × 7) to 35 (5 × 7) servings

Multiplication is also useful to double, triple, and quadruple numbers. To double a number, you multiply the number by 2, to triple a number, you multiply the number by 3, and to quadruple a number, you multiply the number by 4.

Multiplication is used in cooking when you want to end up with more than the recipe makes. Cooks frequently double or triple recipes.

Try the Math Activity to practice doubling and tripling ingredients.

MARVELOUS MULTIPLICATION

MATH ACTIVITY

Materials
pencil
notebook

Procedure
1. Double the following ingredients. Record the answers in your notebook.

    a. 2 pounds carrots

    b. 6 eggs

    c. 5 ounces Swiss cheese

    d. 12 grapes

2. Triple the following ingredients. Record the answers in your notebook.

   a. 3 cups bread flour

   b. 2 teaspoons salt

   c. 4 apples

   d. 6 tablespoons buttermilk

   Check your answers in Appendix A.

○ ○ ○ ○ ○ ○ ○ ○ ○ ○ • • • • • • • • • • • • • • • • • • ○

SANDWICH RECIPES

Each of these recipes makes 1 sandwich. You'll need to double, triple, or quadruple the amount of each ingredient to make 2, 3, or 4 sandwiches.

•••• Three-Cheese Grilled •••• Cheese Sandwich

Instead of using margarine to coat the bread, try mayonnaise. It works well and tastes great. But first, double this recipe by multiplying the amount of each ingredient by 2. Check your answers in Appendix A.

Time
15 minutes

Tools
sandwich spreader or table knife

small nonstick skillet

spatula

Makes
1 sandwich

Ingredients

1 tablespoon low-fat mayonnaise dressing

2 slices whole wheat bread

1 slice American cheese

1 slice Muenster cheese

1 slice Swiss cheese

3 pickle chips

Steps

1. Use the sandwich spreader or table knife to spread the mayonnaise on one side of each slice of bread.

2. Preheat a small nonstick skillet by placing it on a burner set to medium heat for 2 minutes.

3. Place one slice of bread, mayonnaise side down, in the skillet.

4. Layer the 3 slices of cheese on the bread in the skillet. Place the second slice of bread mayonnaise side up on top of the cheese to make your sandwich.

5. Cook the sandwich for 3 to 4 minutes or until the bottom is lightly toasted and golden brown.

6. Use the spatula to turn the sandwich over. Cook the other side about 2 minutes until it is golden brown and the cheese is melted.

7. Lift the sandwich out of the pan and onto a plate. Cut carefully in half. Serve with pickle chips.

• • • • •
Mayonnaise can be used on the bread because, like margarine, it contains fat. Fat prevents the bread from sticking to the pan during cooking.
• • • • •

Dinnertime California···· Burger in a Pocket

Time
20 minutes

Tools
small mixing bowl

wooden spoon

cutting board

paring knife

small nonstick skillet

spatula

sandwich spreader
or table knife

Makes
1 sandwich (2 pita halves)

If you're tired of the same old burger on a bun, stuff your burger and veggies into a pita pocket for a change of pace. But before you begin, triple this recipe to see how much of each ingredient you'd need to make 3 sandwiches. Check Appendix A for the answers.

Ingredients

1 small tomato (2 slices)

1 green leaf lettuce leaf

4 ounces lean ground beef

1 dash salt

1 dash pepper

1 small onion (2 slices)

1 large round pita bread

vegetable oil cooking spray

2 tablespoons low-fat
   mayonnaise dressing

Steps

1. Wash the tomato and lettuce leaf. Set aside to dry.

2. In the bowl, combine the beef, salt, and pepper and mix well with the wooden spoon. Use your hands to shape the beef mixture into a round patty.

3. On the cutting board, use the paring knife to cut 2 slices of tomato.

4. Remove the papery covering from the onion and cut 2 slices of onion. Set the tomato and onion slices aside.

5. Cut the pita round in half to make 2 pieces of bread that look like half moons.

6. Spray a small nonstick skillet with vegetable oil cooking spray.

7. Preheat the skillet by placing it on a burner set to medium heat for 2 minutes.

8. Put the beef burger in the skillet. Cook it for about 6 minutes or until it is browned on the bottom.

9. Turn the burger with the spatula and cook the other side for about 4 minutes or until browned.

10. Remove the burger from the skillet and put it on the cutting board to cool for 5 minutes.

11. While the burger is cooling, use the sandwich spreader or table knife to spread the mayonnaise on the inside of both pita pocket halves.

12. Cut the burger in half and place each half in a pita pocket.

13. Rip the lettuce leaf in half and place a half in each pita pocket. Add the tomato and onion slices to each pocket.

•••••••••••• •••• Tuna and Melted Cheese •••• •••••••••• Croissant Sandwich

Time
25 minutes

Tools
small mixing bowl

fork

table knife

cookie sheet

sandwich spreader

oven mitts

Makes
1 sandwich

This sandwich is great for lunchtime or as a light supper. Before you begin, quadruple this recipe by multiplying the amount of each ingredient by 4. Check your answers in Appendix A.

Ingredients

4 tablespoons canned tuna fish

2 tablespoons low-fat mayonnaise dressing

1 teaspoon dried chives

1 croissant

vegetable oil cooking spray

1 slice American cheese

Steps

1. In the bowl, combine the tuna fish, mayonnaise, and chives and mix together thoroughly with the fork.

2. Use the table knife to split the croissant in half.

3. Look in the oven and make sure there is an oven rack about 4 to 6 inches from the broiler heat source. Turn the oven to broil and preheat for 5 minutes.

4. Spray the cookie sheet with vegetable oil cooking spray.

5. Place the bottom half of the croissant on the cookie sheet. Use the sandwich spreader or table knife to spread the tuna fish on this croissant half.

6. Fold the slice of cheese in half. Cover the tuna with the cheese.

7. Place the cookie sheet under the broiler until the cheese is melted and begins to bubble, about 1 minute. Keep your eye on the sandwich and don't let the cheese brown!

8. Use oven mitts to take the cookie sheet out of the oven. Close the sandwich with the top half of the croissant.

• • • • •
Whenever you use the broiler, don't leave it. Keep an eye on what you are cooking, or at least check it once or twice each minute. The broiler is very hot and cooks foods quickly.
• • • • •

CHAPTER 8

HOW DO YOU CUT AN APPLE-SAUCE RECIPE IN IN HALF?

When a recipe makes more than you want or need, you must divide each ingredient to get a recipe for the right amount. Dividing is the opposite of multiplying. If you multiply 2 × 4 (the factors), the answer is 8 (the product). If you divide the product (8), by either of the factors (2 or 4), the answer is the other factor.

$$2 \times 4 = 8 \qquad 8 \div 2 = 4 \qquad 8 \div 4 = 2$$

Let's look at a pizza that is divided in half (divided by 2) or in thirds (divided by 3).

8 slices ÷ 2 = 4 slices   12 slices ÷ 3 = 4 slices

This recipe for Applesauce makes 8 servings. Let's divide the recipe in half to make 4 servings.

8 Granny Smith or McIntosh apples ÷ 2 = 4 apples

12 tablespoons water ÷ 2 = 6 tablespoons

2 tablespoons cinnamon ÷ 2 = 1 tablespoon

4 tablespoons white sugar ÷ 2 = 2 tablespoons

1 tablespoon brown sugar ÷ 2 = ½ tablespoon

Try the Math Activity to practice dividing ingredients.

DARING DIVISION

Materials
pencil
notebook

Procedure

1. Divide in half (by 2) the following ingredients. Record the answers in your notebook.

    a. 6 eggs

    b. 4 apples

    c. 1 tablespoon parsley

    d. 12 grapes

2. Divide in quarters (by 4) the following ingredients. Record the answers in your notebook.

    a. 4 cups bread flour

    b. 8 teaspoons sugar

    c. 16 ravioli

    d. 20 crackers

Check your answers in Appendix A.

APPLE RECIPES

Divide each of the following recipes as directed. To make sure you divided correctly, check your answers in Appendix A.

Baked Golden Apples and Carrots

Before you begin, divide this recipe in quarters (by 4) to make 2 servings. Try this recipe as a side dish with any chicken entree.

Time
20 minutes to prepare
plus
50 minutes to bake

Tools
cutting board

paring knife

shallow 2-quart baking dish

vegetable peeler

tablespoon

aluminum foil

fork

oven mitts

Makes
8 servings

• • • • •

If you don't like Golden Delicious apples, you can use Red Delicious.

• • • • •

Ingredients

4   medium Golden Delicious apples

12 carrots

4   tablespoons firmly packed brown sugar

½   teaspoon nutmeg

8   teaspoons margarine

Steps

1. Preheat the oven to 350°F.

2. Wash and dry the apples.

3. On the cutting board, use the paring knife to cut the apples in half. Remove the apple cores and seeds. Cut each apple half into 4 pieces.

4. Arrange the apple wedges in two layers around the outside edge of the baking dish.

5. Peel the carrots with the vegetable peeler.

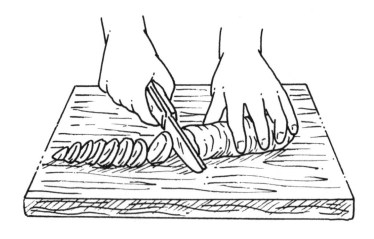

6. On the cutting board, use the paring knife to slice the carrots at an angle into ¼-inch-thick slices. Place the carrot slices in the center of the baking dish.

7. Sprinkle the brown sugar and nutmeg evenly over the apples and carrots. Use a tablespoon to put pieces of margarine on top of the carrots and apples.

8. Cover the dish with aluminum foil.

9. Bake for about 50 minutes, or until the carrots are tender when pierced with a fork. Use oven mitts to remove the dish from the oven.

···· Cherry-Baked Apples ····

Time
10 minutes to prepare
plus
50 to 60 minutes to bake

Tools
cutting board

apple corer

baking pan big enough
to fit the apples

paring knife

spoon

oven mitts

Makes
6 servings

• • • • •

*Red or Golden Delicious,
Granny Smith, and
Rome Beauty apples
are good baking apples.
Choose any of these
types for this recipe.*

• • • • •

*Divide this recipe in thirds (by 3) to make
2 baked apples. Remember to check
Appendix A for the answers.*

Ingredients

6 baking apples

9 tablespoons cherry pie
filling

12 fluid ounces cherry soda

1 cup water

18 pecan pieces

Steps

1. Preheat the oven to 375°F.

2. On the cutting board, use the apple corer to remove
the cores from the apples.

3. Put the apples upright in the baking pan. You may
need to use the paring knife to cut a thin slice off the
bottom of the apples so they sit in the pan without
falling over.

4. Fill the center of each apple with 1½ tablespoons of
cherry pie filling.

5. Drizzle the cherry soda over the apples. Pour the cup of water into the bottom of the pan.

6. Bake for 50 to 60 minutes, or until the apples are soft. During the cooking, spoon the liquid from the bottom of the pan over the apples to keep them moist.

7. Use oven mitts to remove the pan from the oven. Put 4 pecan pieces on top of each apple and serve.

Time
10 minutes

Tools
cutting board

paring knife

toaster

sandwich spreader
or table knife

small bowl

spoon

Makes
4 servings

Divide this recipe in half (by 2) to make 2 servings.

Ingredients

2 small apples

4 English muffins

8 tablespoons light cream cheese

8 tablespoons raisins

2 teaspoons cinnamon

2 teaspoons sugar

Steps

1. On the cutting board, use the paring knife to cut the apples in half. Remove the apple cores and seeds. Cut each apple half into ¼-inch slices.

2. Split open each English muffin to get 8 muffin halves. Toast the halves.

3. Use the sandwich spreader or table knife to spread 1 tablespoon of cream cheese on each muffin half.

4. Arrange 1 tablespoon of raisins around the edge of each muffin half.

5. Arrange sliced apples on top of each muffin in a starburst pattern.

6. In the bowl, mix the cinnamon and sugar with the spoon.

7. Sprinkle the cinnamon sugar over the muffins.

CHAPTER 9

HOW MUCH LETTUCE DO YOU NEED FOR 6 SALADS?

For certain kinds of dishes, you need a recipe and you must follow it precisely. That is surely true when baking cakes, cookies, muffins, and any other baked goods. However, for other kinds of dishes, such as salads, you don't need a recipe. You can estimate how much of each ingredient you'll need.

To estimate means to give an approximate rather than an exact answer. For example, if you know that 3 to 4 cherry tomatoes are needed for one salad, you can estimate that you'll need to buy about 12, or a few more, to make 4 salads. For some practice estimating, try the Math Activity.

EXCELLENT ESTIMATING

MATH ACTIVITY

Materials

pencil

notebook

Food Guide Pyramid (p.167)

Procedure

1. Turn to the Food Guide Pyramid on p. 167. The Food Guide Pyramid gives the number of servings you need each day from the five food groups.

Bread, cereal, rice, and pasta group	6 to 11 servings
Vegetable group	3 to 5 servings
Fruit group	2 to 4 servings
Milk, yogurt, & cheese group	2 to 3 servings
Meats, poultry, fish, dry beans, eggs, and nuts	2 to 3 servings

Estimate how many servings you had yesterday from each group and record it in your notebook. One serving is approximately one slice of bread, one bowl of cereal, ½ cup of rice or pasta, ½ cup of vegetables or fruit, 1 small piece of fresh fruit, 1 cup of juice, and 1 cup of milk or yogurt. Keep in mind that estimating is an approximate, not an exact, answer.

2. Compare how many servings you ate in each food group to the recommended numbers given in the Food Guide Pyramid. Do you eat fewer than the recommended number of servings for any food groups? Do you eat more servings than recommended from any food groups? Which food groups do you need to eat more often?

SALAD RECIPES

For each salad recipe, first decide if you want to make 4 or 6 servings. Then estimate how much of each fruit or salad ingredient you need. Check your estimates in Appendix A.

Fresh Fruit Platter with Yummy Yogurt Dip

One of the best parts of making a fresh fruit and dip platter (besides eating it) is arranging it to look attractive!

Fruit Ingredients

Fresh fruits for dipping, such as apples, bananas, pineapple chunks, any kind of melon, grapes, or strawberries.

Dressing Ingredients

2 8-ounce containers plain low-fat yogurt

¼ cup confectioner's sugar

½ cup heavy cream

Steps

1. Wash the fruit.

2. On the cutting board, use the knife to chop the fruit into bite-size pieces. Arrange the fruit pieces attractively on a serving platter.

3. To make the dip, use the wooden spoon to mix together the yogurt and sugar in one of the bowls.

4. In the other bowl, use the electric mixer to beat the heavy cream until stiff peaks form.

5. Fold the whipped cream into the yogurt mixture with the spatula.

6. Pour the dip into a small serving bowl.

7. Place the dip next to the fruit platter and set out toothpicks for people to use to pick up the fruit.

Time
30 minutes

Tools
knife

cutting board

serving platter

2 medium bowls

wooden spoon

electric mixer

spatula

small serving bowl

toothpicks

Dressing Makes
12 servings

Tortilla 'n' Cheese·····
Fiesta Salad

*The tortilla chips make this salad
really crunchy! Olé!*

Time
20 minutes

Tools
medium salad bowl

cutting board

paring knife

salad tongs

small bowl

whisk

Dressing Makes
4 to 6 servings

• • • • •
*Romaine lettuce has
large, long, dark green
leaves. It is crisp with a
slightly sharp flavor.*
• • • • •

Salad Ingredients

romaine lettuce

tomatoes

tortilla chips

pimento-stuffed olives

shredded sharp cheddar
cheese

Dressing Ingredients

½ cup salsa

½ cup low-fat Italian salad
dressing

Steps

1. Wash and dry the lettuce and tomatoes.

2. Rip the romaine lettuce into large bite-size pieces and
place in the salad bowl.

3. On the cutting board, use the paring knife to cut the
tomatoes into wedges. Also, slice the olives into ¼-inch
slices.

4. Put the tomatoes, tortilla chips, and olives in the salad
bowl and use salad tongs to mix well.

5. In the small bowl, whisk together the salsa and Italian dressing until smooth and creamy. Lightly drizzle half the dressing over the salad and toss the salad using the salad tongs.

6. Sprinkle the shredded cheese over the top of the salad.

7. Use the rest of the dressing as a dip for more tortilla chips.

PART 3

FRACTIONS AND PERCENTS

You've already seen loads of fractions and used them in your cooking. When a recipe calls for ¾ cup of brown sugar and ½ teaspoon salt, you know what to do. But what if you need to add fractions and play with percents? We'll show you how, so that you can be an expert Math Chef!

CHAPTER 10
WHAT'S ⅓ OF A WAFFLE?

If you split a whole waffle equally in half, each piece is ½ of a waffle. If you split a waffle into 3 equal pieces, each piece is ⅓ of a waffle. Thus a **fraction**, such as ½ or ⅓, is a number that names part of a whole.

The top number in a fraction is called the **numerator**. The bottom number in a fraction is called the **denominator**. To add fractions, the denominators must be the same. When you add fractions with the same denominators, you add only the numerators, and leave the denominators the same. Fractions and whole numbers are always added separately.

For example:

$$\frac{1}{4} + \frac{2}{4} = \frac{3}{4} \qquad \frac{4}{5} + \frac{1}{5} = \frac{5}{5} = 1$$

$$1\frac{1}{3} + 2\frac{1}{3} = 3\frac{2}{3} \qquad \frac{9}{10} + \frac{3}{10} = \frac{12}{10}$$

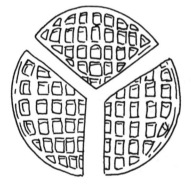

A fraction with the same numerator and denominator is equal to 1. Sometimes when you add fractions, the answer is greater than 1. In the last example above, the answer is $\frac{12}{10}$. $\frac{12}{10}$ is called an **improper fraction**. An improper fraction has a numerator that is greater than its denominator. Follow these steps to change an improper fraction to its simplest form, a whole number and a fraction.

1. Divide the numerator by the denominator.
$\frac{12}{10} = 1$ with a remainder of 2

2. Write the remainder as a fraction.
$\frac{2}{10}$

3. $\frac{12}{10} = 1\frac{2}{10}$.

Fractions should always be reduced to their simplest form. A fraction is in its simplest form when both the numerator and denominator have no common factors other than 1. To reduce a fraction to its simplest form, divide both the numerator and denominator by their greatest common factor. For example:

$$\frac{2}{10} = \frac{2 \div 2}{10 \div 2} = \frac{1}{5}$$

Like fractions, decimals are also used to represent part of a whole. A **decimal** is a number with one or more places to the right of a decimal point, such as 2.5. The numbers to the left of the decimal point are whole numbers. The numbers to the right represent tenths, hundredths, and so on. The number 2.5 is equal to 2 and $\frac{5}{10}$, which can be reduced to $2\frac{1}{2}$.

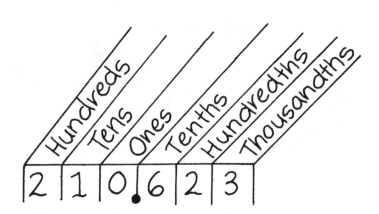

MATH ACTIVITY

Materials
pencil
notebook

Procedure

You plan to bake chocolate chip cookies and chocolate chip scones for a school bake sale. Some of the ingredients are needed in both recipes. Do you have enough? Write a list in your notebook of how much you need by adding the amounts needed of each of the following ingredients.

Chocolate Chip Cookies	Chocolate Chip Scones
a. 1¾ cups brown sugar	¼ cup brown sugar
b. ¾ teaspoon vanilla extract	¼ teapoon vanilla extract
c. ½ teaspoon salt	½ teaspoon salt
d. 2 cups all-purpose flour	2½ cups all-purpose flour

Check your answers in Appendix A.

SNACK RECIPES

To make the following snack recipes, you'll need to add fractions for the ingredients shown in **boldface** type. Check your answers in Appendix A.

Hiking Munchies

Make this recipe up before you go on your next hike!

Ingredients

1¼ + ¾ = ? cups low-fat granola cereal

1½ cups dry-roasted peanuts

1 cup pretzel sticks

1 cup cheese crackers

¾ cup raisins

Steps

1. Measure the ingredients one at a time and put them in the bowl.

2. Mix all ingredients together gently with the wooden spoon. Place 1 cup of the mixture in each plastic bag.

Time
15 minutes

Tools
large bowl

wooden spoon

6 resealable plastic bags

Makes
6 1-cup servings

• • • • •
Peanut plants are unusual because they flower above the ground but their fruits (the peanuts) grow below the ground.
• • • • •

Fraction Pretzels

Pretzels don't have to be twisted. Using this recipe, you can make your own pretzels and shape them into numbers!

Time
2½ to 3 hours

Tools
2 cookie sheets

large mixing bowl

wooden spoon

thermometer

2 medium mixing bowls

cutting board

pastry brush

kitchen towel

paring knife

small bowl

fork

oven mitts

Makes
12 fraction pretzels

• • • • •
Yeast is a fungus that makes bread dough rise or expand. Lukewarm water enables the yeast to grow. If the water is too hot, the yeast will die. If the water is too cold, the yeast will freeze!
• • • • •

Ingredients

vegetable oil cooking spray

⅔ + ⅔ = ? cups luke-warm water

1 tablespoon sugar

1 package active dry yeast

1 tablespoon vegetable oil

2 cups all-purpose flour

1¼ cups whole wheat flour

1 teaspoon salt

1 teaspoon vegetable oil

1 egg

2 teaspoons water

2 teaspoons coarse salt

extra flour for kneading

Steps

1. Preheat the oven to 425°F.

2. Spray the cookie sheets with vegetable oil cooking spray.

3. Put the water in the large mixing bowl. Use a thermometer to make sure the water temperature is between 105 to 115°F.

4. Add the sugar to the warm water and stir with the wooden spoon until the sugar dissolves.

5. Sprinkle the yeast over the sugar and water mixture. **Do not stir the yeast.** Let the yeast mixture stand for about 5 minutes until it looks foamy.

6. Add the 1 tablespoon of oil to the water.

7. In one of the medium mixing bowls, combine the all-purpose flour, whole wheat flour, and salt.

8. Add the flour mixture to the liquid ingredients in small amounts. Stir well after each addition until the mixture forms a dough.

9. Lightly sprinkle about 2 tablespoons of flour on a cutting board or other surface. Put the dough on the floured surface and knead it for 8 to 10 minutes. Knead by pressing the dough out, then folding it in half towards you. Give the dough a quarter turn after each fold and start again. When you've finished kneading, roll the dough into a ball.

10. Use the pastry brush to lightly brush the other medium mixing bowl with the 1 teaspoon of vegetable oil.

11. Put the ball of dough in the oiled bowl. Turn it over in the bowl so that the dough has a thin coating of oil all over it.

12. Cover the bowl with a damp kitchen towel and put it in a warm place for 1 hour to allow the dough to rise.

13. When the dough has risen, punch it down in the bowl by pulling it up on all sides and then folding it over the center and pressing down.

14. Place the dough on the cutting board. Use the paring knife to divide the dough into 12 equal portions.

15. Roll the dough pieces into 12-inch strips. Cut each 12-inch strip into 2 6-inch strips. Shape 18 strips into numbers and use the last 6 strips to make dashes for your fractions. Place the shaped pieces on the cookie sheets.

16. In the small bowl, mix the egg with the 1 teaspoon of water and beat well with a fork.

17. Lightly brush the pretzels with the egg wash. Sprinkle the pretzels lightly with salt.

18. Bake the pretzels for 15 to 20 minutes or until they are golden brown. Use oven mitts to remove the cookie sheets from the oven.

• • • • •
An egg wash is simply an egg mixed with water. It is frequently used in baking to give the baked product a shine.
• • • • •

19. Allow the pretzels to cool for 10 minutes before removing them from the sheets. Serve warm or wrap tightly in plastic once completely cooled.

*If you want a healthy snack with
a lot of crunch, make this granola and
pack it for school and trips.*

Time
18 to 20 minutes
to prepare
plus
1 hour to cool

Tools
cookie sheet

large bowl

wooden spoon

oven mitts

sandwich bags

Makes
8 ½-cup servings

Ingredients

vegetable oil cooking spray

⅓ + ⅔ = ? cup rolled oats

⅓ cup wheat germ

¼ cup shredded coconut

½ cup sunflower seeds

¼ cup powdered milk

¼ cup raisins

½ teaspoon cinnamon

½ teaspoon nutmeg

¼ cup honey

2 tablespoons vegetable oil

1 teaspoon vanilla extract

Steps

1. Preheat the oven to 375°F.

2. Spray the cookie sheet with vegetable oil cooking spray.

3. In the bowl, mix together the rolled oats, wheat germ, shredded coconut, sunflower seeds, powdered milk, raisins, cinnamon, and nutmeg, using the wooden spoon.

4. Add the honey, vegetable oil, and vanilla extract to the mixture. Stir well until the honey covers all of the dry ingredients.

5. Press the mixture flat on the sprayed cookie sheet.

6. Bake the granola for 8 to 10 minutes until it is toasted, or light brown in color. Use oven mitts to remove the cookie sheet from the oven.

7. Let the granola cool on the cookie sheet for about 1 hour.

8. Put the granola into sandwich bags and pack in lunch boxes for school.

•••••••••••••• •••• Peachy Snack Rolls •••• •••••••••••••

Time
20 minutes to prepare
plus
3 hours to cook

Tools
cookie sheet

blender

2-cup liquid measuring cup

sandwich spreader
or table knife

oven mitts

spatula

cutting board

paring knife

resealable plastic
sandwich bags

Makes
10 fruit rolls

If you like fruit rolls, here's a recipe to try out.

Ingredients

vegetable oil cooking spray

9 + 1½ = ? ounces frozen peaches, thawed

1 tablespoon lemon juice

¼ teaspoon nutmeg

Steps

1. Preheat the oven to 175°F.

2. Spray the cookie sheet with vegetable oil cooking spray.

3. Put the peaches, lemon juice, and nutmeg in the blender container and blend until smooth.

4. Measure 2 cups of the peach mixture.

5. Use the sandwich spreader or table knife to spread the fruit mixture thinly over the cookie sheet.

6. Bake with the oven door slightly open for about 3 hours. Every 30 minutes, use oven mitts to remove the sheet from the oven and check to see if the peach roll is dry enough to peel off the cookie sheet. If it is still wet after 3 hours, use the spatula to flip it over and return it to the oven for about 10 minutes more.

7. Take the cookie sheet out of the oven, using oven mitts. Peel the peach roll from the cookie sheet and place it on the cutting board.

8. Cut the peach roll crosswise into strips with the paring knife. Roll up the strips and store in plastic bags.

CHAPTER 11

WHAT'S THE PERCENT OF MARGARINE IN A MUFFIN?

A percent is a type of **ratio**, which is a comparison of two related numbers. A **percent** is a ratio that always compares some number to 100. For example, 30 percent (30%) means 30 compared to 100, as shown here.

Ratio = $^{30}\!/_{100}$ or .3

Percent = 30%

Professional bakers use percents called baker's percents. **Baker's percents** tell them the amount of each ingredient in the recipe compared to the amount of flour in the recipe. For example, if a recipe uses 4 ounces of margarine and 10 ounces of flour, the baker's percent will

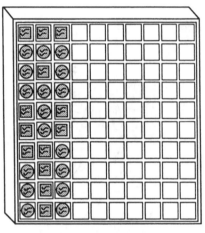

be 40%, as shown below. You can convert any ratio to a percent using the following two steps.

1. Divide the denominator of the ratio into its numerator.

$$\frac{\text{Weight of ingredient}}{\text{Weight of flour}} = \frac{4 \text{ ounces}}{10 \text{ ounces}} = .4$$

2. Multiply the answer from step 1 by 100 to get a percent.

.4 × 100 = 40%

Do the following Math Activity to practice calculating percents.

MUFFIN MADNESS

Materials

pencil

notebook

2 cups margarine

4½ cups all-purpose flour

4½ cups whole wheat flour

2 cups powdered milk

⅓ cup baking powder

¼ cup sugar

1 tablespoon salt

cutting board

table knife

large bowl

pastry blender

wooden spoon

Procedure

1. You are going to use the ingredients listed here to make Basic Muffin Mix. With this mix, you can make any of the 5 muffin recipes given in this chapter.

2. Before you make the mix, calculate the percent of margarine (2 cups) compared to the 9 cups total flour. Check your answer in Appendix A.

3. Now, make the mix:

a. On the cutting board, use a table knife to cut the margarine into small pieces. Put the pieces in the large bowl.

b. Add the all-purpose and whole wheat flours.

c. Use the pastry blender to cut through the margarine and dry ingredients. Keep cutting, by rocking the blender back and forth, until the flour and margarine mixture resembles the size of peas.

d. Add the powdered milk, baking powder, sugar, and salt. Stir with the wooden spoon until thoroughly blended. The recipe makes 14 cups, enough to make all the muffin recipes in this chapter.

e. Place the finished muffin mix in an airtight container and refrigerate. It will keep in the refrigerator for up to 5 weeks.

MUFFIN RECIPES

Some of the muffin recipes have a baker's percent question for you to answer. Those recipes each have two ingredients in **boldface** type. Before you begin the recipe, calculate the baker's percent in those recipes. Check your answer in Appendix A, then make some great muffins!

············ Banana Blaster Muffins ············

BAKER'S PERCENT QUESTION:
What is the percent of chocolate minichips compared to muffin mix?

Time
15 minutes to prepare
plus
15 to 18 minutes to bake

Tools
muffin pan

2 medium bowls

masher

wooden spoon

oven mitts

cooling rack

rubber spatula

Makes
12 muffins

Ingredients

vegetable oil cooking spray

3 cups Basic Muffin Mix

1 tablespoon sugar

2 ripe bananas

1 egg

2 tablespoons honey

1 teaspoon vanilla extract

1 cup chocolate minichips

Steps

1. Preheat oven to 400°F.

2. Spray muffin pan with vegetable oil cooking spray.

3. Put muffin mix and sugar in a medium bowl. Stir well with the wooden spoon. Set aside.

4. In the other bowl, mash the bananas with the masher. Add the egg, honey, and vanilla extract and stir.

5. Add the banana mixture to the bowl with the muffin mix. Stir with the wooden spoon to combine just until you don't see any dry mix.

6. Use the wooden spoon to fold in the chocolate minichips.

• • • • •
Use a gentle over-and-under motion when you fold in the chocolate minichips.
• • • • •

7. Fill the cups in the muffin pan evenly, so they are about ⅔ full.

8. Bake for 15 to 18 minutes, or until muffins are golden brown.

9. Use oven mitts to remove the muffin pan from the oven. Place the pan on the cooling rack and let cool for 5 minutes.

10. Use the rubber spatula to loosen the muffins and remove from pan.

Whole Wheat Honey and Date Muffins

Dates are the fruits of a type of palm tree.
You can buy dates either fresh or dried.
They are very sweet.

Time
15 minutes to prepare
plus
18 to 20 minutes to bake

Tools
muffin pan

2 medium bowls

wooden spoon

wire whip

oven mitts

cooling rack

rubber spatula

Makes
12 muffins

Ingredients

vegetable oil cooking spray

2½ cups Basic Muffin Mix

½ cup old-fashioned oatmeal

1 egg

2 tablespoons honey

¾ cup water

1 cup pitted dates, chopped

½ cup walnuts, chopped

Steps

1. Preheat oven to 400°F.

2. Spray the muffin pan with vegetable oil cooking spray.

3. Put the muffin mix and oatmeal into a medium bowl. Stir well with the wooden spoon.

4. In the other bowl, whisk together the egg, honey, and water.

5. Add the egg mixture to the bowl with the muffin mix. Use the wooden spoon to combine just until you don't see any dry mix.

6. Use the wooden spoon to fold in the dates and nuts.

7. Fill the cups in the muffin pan evenly so they are about ⅔ full.

8. Bake for 18 to 20 minutes, or until muffins are golden brown.

9. Use oven mitts to remove the muffin pan from the oven. Place the pan on the cooling rack and let cool for 5 minutes.

10. Use the rubber spatula to loosen the muffins and remove from pan.

• • • • •
Dried dates are dark brown in color and are very sweet and chewy. The date palm tree ripens fruit only in warm, dry climates such as that of California and Northern Africa.
• • • • •

Time
15 minutes to prepare
plus
18 to 20 minutes to bake

Tools
muffin pan

2 medium bowls

wooden spoon

wire whip

oven mitts

cooling rack

rubber spatula

Makes
12 muffins

PB, of course, stands for peanut butter, a favorite food of both children and adults. The surprise in this muffin is the jam in the middle.

Ingredients

vegetable oil cooking spray
2½ cups Basic Muffin Mix
½ cup wheat germ
2 tablespoons sugar
1 teaspoon cinnamon

1 egg
⅓ cup peanut butter
1 cup water
1 teaspoon vanilla extract
½ cup raspberry or strawberry jam

Steps

1. Preheat oven to 400°F.

2. Spray muffin pan with vegetable oil cooking spray.

3. Put the muffin mix, wheat germ, sugar, and cinnamon in a medium bowl. Stir well with a wooden spoon.

4. In the other bowl, whisk together the egg, peanut butter, water, and vanilla extract.

5. Add the egg mixture to the bowl with the muffin mix. Use the wooden spoon to combine just until you don't see any dry mix.

6. Place 1 heaping tablespoon of batter on the bottom of each cup in the muffin pan.

7. Add 2 teaspoons jam on top of the batter in each cup. Cover the jam with the remaining batter so that the cups are about ⅔ filled.

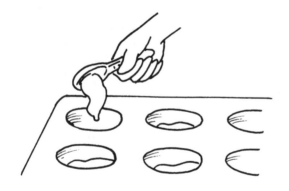

8. Bake for 18 to 20 minutes, or until muffins are golden brown.

9. Use oven mitts to remove the pan from the oven. Place the pan on a cooling rack and let cool for 5 minutes.

10. Loosen the muffins with a rubber spatula and remove from pan.

···· Radical Peach Muffins ····

Time
15 minutes to prepare
plus
18 to 20 minutes to bake

Tools
muffin pan

cutting board

paring knife

2 medium bowls

wooden spoon

masher

oven mitts

cooling rack

rubber spatula

Makes
12 muffins

Canned peach halves are delicious inside a warm muffin. Try it and see!

Ingredients

vegetable oil cooking spray
6 canned peach halves
3 cups Basic Muffin Mix
2 tablespoons sugar
1 dash cinnamon

2 ripe bananas
1 egg
1 teaspoon vanilla extract
⅓ cup water

Steps

1. Preheat oven to 400°F.
2. Spray muffin pan with vegetable oil cooking spray.
3. On the cutting board, use the paring knife to cut the peaches into bite-size pieces.
4. Put muffin mix, sugar, and cinnamon into a medium bowl. Stir well with the wooden spoon. Set aside.
5. In the other bowl, mash the bananas with the masher. Add the egg, vanilla extract, and water and stir with the wooden spoon.
6. Add the banana mixture to the bowl with the muffin mix. Use the wooden spoon to combine just until you don't see any dry mix.
7. Fold in the peach pieces.
8. Fill the cups in the muffin pan evenly, so they are about ⅔ full.
9. Bake for 15 to 18 minutes, or until muffins are golden brown.
10. Use the oven mitts to remove the muffin pan from the oven. Place the pan on the cooling rack and let cool for 5 minutes.
11. Use the rubber spatula to loosen the muffins and remove them from pan.

•••• Munchin' Crunchin' ••••
Butterscotch Muffins

BAKER'S PERCENT QUESTION:
What is the percent of butterscotch morsels
compared to muffin mix?

Time
15 minutes to prepare
plus
18 minutes to bake

Ingredients

vegetable oil cooking spray
3 cups Basic Muffin Mix
2 tablespoons sugar
1 egg

1 teaspoon vanilla extract
⅓ cup peanut butter
¾ cup water
1 cup butterscotch morsels

Tools
muffin pan
medium bowl
fork
small bowl
wire whip
wooden spoon
oven mitts
cooling rack
rubber spatula

Steps

1. Preheat oven to 400°F.

2. Spray the muffin pan with vegetable oil cooking spray.

3. Put the muffin mix and sugar in the medium bowl. Toss with the fork to combine.

4. In the small bowl, whisk together the egg, vanilla extract, peanut butter, and water.

5. Add the egg mixture to the bowl with the muffin mix. Use the wooden spoon to combine just until you don't see any dry mix.

6. Fold in the butterscotch morsels.

7. Fill the cups in the muffin pan evenly, so they are about ⅔ full.

8. Bake for 15 to 18 minutes, or until muffins are golden brown.

9. Use the oven mitts to remove the muffin pan from the oven. Place the pan on a cooling rack and let cool for 5 minutes.

10. Use the rubber spatula to loosen the muffins and remove from pan.

PART 4

GEOMETRY

Geometry is the branch of math that has to do with points, lines, and shapes. Geometrical shapes—such as squares, rectangles, triangles, and circles—abound in the kitchen. Imagine cookies, baking pans, raviolis—even crackers—without geometry!

CHAPTER 12
WHAT'S THE AREA OF A BROWNIE?

The **area** of any square or rectangle is the number of squares with sides equal to one unit that the square or rectangle contains. For example, the rectangle shown is 5 units by 2 units and contains exactly 10 squares with sides equal to one unit. We say that the area of this rectangle is 10 square units, also written 10 units^2.

length = 5

width = 2

You don't need to draw a rectangle or square every time you need to calculate area, however. To find the area of a square or rectangle, you multiply its length times its width. In the rectangle here, you multiply its length, 5 units, by its width, 2 units, to get its area, 10 square units.

Let's use the formula for area to calculate the area of some brownies.

width = 3 inches

length = 4 inches

length × width = area
4 inches × 3 inches = 12 square inches

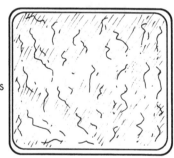

width = 10 centimeters

length = 10 centimeters

length × width = area
10 centimeters × 10 centimeters = 100 square centimeters

For more practice, try the Math Activity.

SPECTACULAR SQUARES AND RECTANGLES

Materials

pencil

notebook

pictures below

Procedure

Calculate the area of the following pans used for baking and cooking in restaurants. Check your answers in Appendix A.

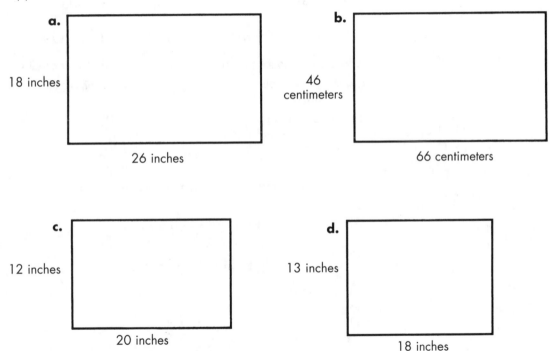

a.

18 inches

26 inches

b.

46 centimeters

66 centimeters

c.

12 inches

20 inches

d.

13 inches

18 inches

BAR COOKIE RECIPES

Before you begin each of these recipes, calculate the area of the baking pan. (The pans are in **boldface** type in the list of tools.) Check your answers in Appendix A.

Double-Cool Brownie and Cream Bars

Time
25 minutes to prepare plus
45 to 50 minutes to bake, and 1 hour to cool

Tools
9-inch square baking pan

medium saucepan

2 wooden spoons

2 medium bowls

small bowl

wire whip

electric mixer

rubber spatula

oven mitts

Makes
18 3-inch × 1½-inch brownies

vegetable oil cooking spray

1 cup (2 sticks) margarine

4 1-ounce squares semisweet chocolate

2 cups sugar

1½ cups all-purpose flour

4 eggs

1 teaspoon salt

1 teaspoon baking powder

1 tablespoon vanilla extract

These brownies are doubly good because

¼ cup confectioner's sugar

2 tablespoons softened margarine

1 3-ounce package cream cheese, softened at room temperature for 1 hour

1 tablespoon all-purpose flour

½ teaspoon vanilla extract

of a delicious filling in the middle.

Brownie Ingredients

Filling Ingredients

Steps
1. Preheat the oven to 350°F.
2. Spray the baking pan with vegetable oil cooking spray.
3. Put the margarine and the semisweet chocolate squares in the saucepan.
4. Cook over medium heat, stirring constantly, with the

wooden spoon until the margarine and chocolate melt. Turn off the heat and set aside.

5. In a medium bowl, use the other wooden spoon to combine the sugar and flour.

6. In the small bowl, whisk the eggs together.

7. Add the salt, baking powder, and vanilla extract to the eggs. Whisk again.

8. Add the egg mixture and the melted margarine and chocolate to the flour mixture and stir until well combined, about 50 strokes.

9. Spread about half the brownie mixture in the sprayed baking pan.

10. To make the filling, use the electric mixer, on medium speed, to beat the sugar and margarine together in the second medium bowl.

11. Add the softened cream cheese and continue to beat until smooth.

12. Slowly mix in the flour and vanilla extract. Beat on medium speed for about 2 minutes.

13. Pour the filling over the brownie mixture in the baking pan. Spread evenly with the rubber spatula.

14. Spoon the remaining brownie mixture over the filling. Spread with the rubber spatula.

15. Bake for 45 to 50 minutes, or until firm.

16. Use the oven mitts to remove the pan from the oven. Let the brownies cool for at least 1 hour.

17. Cut the brownies into 18 3-inch by 1½-inch bars.

Time
60 minutes
plus
2 hours to chill

Tools
**9-inch square
baking pan**

large bowl

electric mixer

wooden spoon

1 gallon resealable
plastic bag

rolling pin

oven mitts

medium bowl

rubber spatula

Makes
18 3-inch × 1½-inch bars

•••••

*Cheesecake is a rich,
creamy dessert. The
main ingredient of
cheesecake is cream
cheese, cottage cheese,
ricotta cheese, or
some combination
of these cheeses.*

•••••

*If you like regular cheesecake, you'll love
these rectangular cheesecake bars.*

Cheesecake Ingredients

vegetable oil cooking spray

⅓ cup (5⅓ tablespoons)
margarine, softened

½ cup dark brown sugar

1 cup all-purpose flour

½ cup finely chopped walnuts

Filling Ingredients

1 8-ounce package cream
cheese, softened at room
temperature for 1 hour

¼ cup confectioner's sugar

1 egg

2 tablespoons milk

2 tablespoons lemon juice

1 teaspoon vanilla extract

½ cup chocolate minichips

Steps

1. Preheat the oven to 350°F.

2. Spray the baking pan with vegetable oil cooking
spray.

3. In the large bowl, use the electric mixer to beat the
margarine and brown sugar together at a medium
speed until well-blended.

4. Use the wooden spoon to slowly stir the flour into the
margarine and brown sugar mixture.

5. Place the chopped walnuts in the plastic bag, making
sure to press the air out of the bag before closing.

6. Roll the rolling pin over the bag of walnuts until the
nuts are finely crushed. Stir the crushed walnuts into
the flour mixture.

7. Measure 1 cup of the flour mixture and set aside.
Press the remaining flour mixture evenly in the bottom
of baking pan.

8. Bake for 8 to 10 minutes until lightly golden. Use the oven mitts to remove the pan from the oven. Leave the oven on.

9. While the flour mixture is baking, make the filling. In the medium bowl, use the electric mixer to beat together the cream cheese and sugar at medium speed. Beat until smooth.

10. Put the mixer on the lowest speed, and add the egg, milk, lemon juice, and vanilla extract to the cheese mixture.

11. Use a wooden spoon to fold in the chocolate chips.

12. Pour the cheese mixture over the warm crust. Spread it evenly with the rubber spatula. Sprinkle the remaining 1 cup of the flour mixture over the cheese mixture.

13. Bake for 30 minutes or until firm and lightly golden brown. Use oven mitts to remove the pan from the oven.

14. Let the pan cool at room temperature for 30 minutes, then place it in refrigerator for 2 hours.

15. To serve, cut into rectangles and remove from the pan.

Cinnamon Strawberry Breakfast Squares

Time
20 minutes to prepare
plus
50 minutes to bake

Tools
9- × 13-inch baking pan

medium bowl

electric mixer

rubber spatula

1 gallon resealable plastic bag

rolling pin

spatula

oven mitts

Makes
12 3-inch × 3-inch squares (approximate)

Try these for breakfast or anytime! They are especially easy to pack with your lunch.

Ingredients

vegetable oil cooking spray

1 cup sugar

1 cup (2 sticks) margarine, softened at room temperature for 1 hour

2½ cups all-purpose flour

1 egg

1 teaspoon cinnamon

1½ cups chopped walnuts

1 12-ounce jar strawberry preserves

Steps

1. Preheat the oven to 350°F.

2. Spray the baking pan with vegetable oil cooking spray.

3. In the medium bowl, use the electric mixer on low speed to slowly beat the sugar into the margarine. Beat until the mixture is creamy.

4. Keeping the electric mixer on low speed, carefully add the flour, egg, and cinnamon to the margarine mixture. Mix until combined. Scrape the mixture down from the sides of the bowl occasionally with the rubber spatula.

5. Place the chopped walnuts in the plastic bag, making sure to press the air out of the bag before closing.

6. Roll the rolling pin over the bag of walnuts. Roll until the nuts are finely crushed. Add the crushed walnuts to the flour mixture.

7. Use your hands to mix the flour mixture until it is well combined.

8. Measure 1½ cups of the flour mixture and set aside. Press the remaining flour mixture evenly into the baking pan.

9. Use the spatula to spread the strawberry preserves evenly over the flour mixture.

10. Sprinkle the remaining 1½ cups of the flour mixture over the strawberry preserves.

11. Bake for 50 minutes, or until lightly golden.

12. Use the oven mitts to remove the pan from the oven. Let cool for about 20 minutes.

13. Cut into 3-inch squares.

Luscious Lemon Squares

Time
20 minutes to prepare
plus
40 minutes to bake
and 1 hour to cool

Tools
8-inch square pan

small bowl

wooden spoon

medium bowl

wire whip

oven mitts

sifter

Makes
16 2-inch squares

Here's another filled bar cookie that is sure to please your friends and family.

Crust Ingredients

vegetable oil cooking spray

½ cup (1 stick) margarine, softened at room temperature for 1 hour

¼ cup sugar

1⅓ cups all-purpose flour

Filling Ingredients

2 eggs

¾ cup confectioner's sugar

2 tablespoons all-purpose flour

¼ teaspoon baking powder

3 tablespoons lemon juice

1 tablespoon confectioner's sugar for sprinkling

Steps

1. Preheat the oven to 350°F.

2. Spray the baking pan with vegetable oil cooking spray.

3. In the small bowl, use a wooden spoon to mix the margarine and sugar together by pressing them against the side of the bowl until they are well mixed and look creamy.

4. Slowly add the flour to the margarine mixture until it is well blended.

5. Knead the flour mixture together for about 1 minute until it forms a dough.

6. Press the dough evenly on the bottom of the baking pan.

7. Bake for about 20 minutes to form a crust.

8. While the crust is baking, make the lemon filling. In the medium bowl, whisk the eggs and the confectioner's sugar together.

9. With the whisk or wooden spoon, slowly mix the flour, baking powder, and lemon juice into the egg mixture until well combined.

10. Use the oven mitts to remove the baking pan from the oven. Leave the oven on.

11. Pour the filling over the baked crust.

12. Bake for 20 minutes, or until the filling is firm. With the oven mitts, remove the pan from the oven. Let cool for about 20 minutes.

13. Cut into 2-inch squares and remove from the pan.

14. Allow the bars to cool for an additional hour.

15. Use the sifter to sprinkle the remaining confectioner's sugar over the bars before serving.

Microwave Butterscotch Applesauce Bars

Time
10 minutes to prepare,
8 minutes to microwave,
plus
15 minutes to cool

Tools
**200 millimeter
(8-inch) square
glass pan**

1 gallon resealable
plastic bag

rolling pin

medium bowl

wooden spoon

oven mitts

Makes
16 2-inch squares

• • • • •
*Butterscotch is
made by cooking
margarine or butter
with brown sugar.*
• • • • •

*If you want to make something sweet
quickly and easily, try these bars!*

Ingredients

vegetable oil cooking spray

3 cups vanilla wafers

½ cup raisins

1 cup butterscotch morsels

¼ cup wheat germ

2 cups applesauce

½ cup chopped nuts or
sunflower seeds (optional)

Steps

1. Spray the bottom of the glass pan with vegetable oil cooking spray.

2. Place the wafers in the plastic bag, making sure to press the air out of the bag before closing.

3. Roll the rolling pin over the bag of wafers until the wafers are crushed into large chunks.

4. Put half of the crushed wafers evenly in the glass pan.

5. In the medium bowl, use the wooden spoon to mix the raisins, butterscotch morsels, wheat germ, and applesauce. Add nuts or sunflower seeds if desired.

6. Spread the applesauce mixture over the wafers in the pan.

7. Press the rest of the crushed wafers evenly over the applesauce mixture.

8. Microwave at full power (high) for 8 minutes. Use oven mitts to remove the pan from the microwave.

9. Let cool for at least 15 minutes before cutting into 2-inch squares and serving. Store any leftovers in the refrigerator.

WHAT'S THE DIAMETER OF A CUPCAKE?

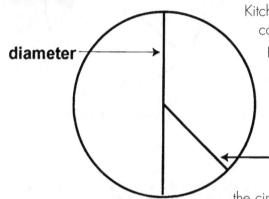

diameter

radius

Kitchens are full of circles, from cupcakes, cookies, and pies to the round pans and plates we use for cooking and eating. Circles are different from any other figure because all of the points on a circle are the same distance from the center. A diameter is a line segment that passes through the center of a circle and has both end points on the circle. A **diameter** cuts the circle exactly in half. A radius is a line segment that joins the center of the circle with any point on the edge of the circle.

A **radius** is always equal to one-half the the length of the diameter of the circle. To calculate the radius, use the formula

$$\text{radius } (r) = \frac{\text{diameter } (d)}{2}.$$

For example:

$$\text{diameter} = 8 \text{ inches}$$

$$\text{radius} = \frac{d}{2}$$

$$\text{radius} = \frac{8 \text{ inches}}{2}$$

$$\text{radius} = 4 \text{ inches}$$

If you know the radius, you can calculate the diameter by doubling the radius (multipling the radius by 2). The formula for calculating diameter is diameter $(d) = 2$ radius (r).

Use the formulas for calculating diameter and radius to determine the missing number from the two plates on the top of page 134. Check Appendix A for the answers.

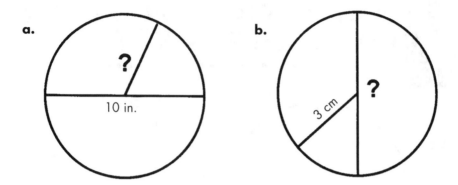

a.

? 10 in.

b.

3 cm ?

Try the Math Activity for some more practice.

MATH ACTIVITY SENSATIONAL CIRCLES

Materials
pencil
can or plate
sheet of white paper
scissors
ruler
notebook

Procedure

1. Trace around the outside of the can or plate onto the white sheet of paper. Cut out the circle with the scissors.

2. Fold the paper circle in half twice. The point where the two folds—or diameters—cross is the exact center of the circle.

3. Use the ruler to measure the diameter in both inches and centimeters. Record in your notebook.

4. Now that you know the diameter, calculate the radius in both inches and centimeters. Remember, $r = \frac{d}{2}$.

5. Next, use your ruler to draw a radius from the center of the circle (where the two folds cross) to any point on the outline of the circle.

6. Measure the radius to make sure it is the same as the radius you calculated.

DESSERT RECIPES

Before you begin each of the cake and tart recipes, calculate the diameter and/or radius of the pans and other tools that are in **boldface** type in the list of tools.

•••••• •••• Nutty Carrot-Top Cupcakes •••• ••••••••

Time
25 minutes to prepare
plus
20 to 25 minutes to bake
plus
1 hour cooling time

Tools
2 muffin pans

paper cupcake cups

2 large bowls

wooden spoon

wire whip

vegetable peeler

grater

ice cream scoop or
serving spoon

oven mitts

cooling rack

sandwich spreader or
table knife

Makes
24 cupcakes

Use the same procedure as in the Math Activity to determine the diameter and radius of the bottom of a cupcake cup.

Ingredients

2 cups all-purpose flour

2 cups sugar

1 teaspoon salt

2 teaspoons baking soda

1 teaspoon cinnamon

½ teaspoon ground nutmeg

½ teaspoon allspice

1½ cups vegetable oil

3 eggs

2 teaspoons vanilla extract

½ cup crushed pineapple

4 large carrots

1 cup chopped walnuts

1 cup raisins

1 cup any flavor ready-to-use frosting or Ultimate Butternut Frosting (page 138)

Steps

1. Preheat the oven to 350°F.

2. Line the muffin pans with the paper cupcake cups. Set aside.

3. In a large bowl, use a wooden spoon to mix together the flour, sugar, salt, baking soda, cinnamon, nutmeg, and allspice.

4. In the other large bowl, whisk together the oil, eggs, vanilla extract, and crushed pineapple. Set both bowls aside.

5. Wash and dry the carrots. Carefully peel the carrots with the vegetable peeler.

6. Grate the carrots on the large-holed side of the grater until you have 2 cups of grated carrots.

7. Add the grated carrots to the oil mixture and mix well with the wooden spoon.

8. Add the oil mixture all at once to the flour mixture and mix with the wooden spoon until well blended.

9. Carefully stir in the chopped walnuts and raisins.

10. Use an ice cream scoop to fill each muffin cup ⅔ full of batter.

11. Bake for 20 to 25 minutes, or until golden brown. Use the oven mitts to remove the pans from the oven and place on the cooling rack. Let the pans cool for 15 minutes.

12. Remove the cupcakes from the pan and let cool for at least 1 hour.

13. Use the sandwich spreader or table knife to ice the cupcakes with a ready-to-use frosting or Ultimate Butternut Frosting, which follows.

• • • • •
Dip the spreader into warm water for a few minutes before icing the cupcakes
• • • • •

········ ···· Ultimate Butternut Frosting ···· ········

Time
15 minutes

Tools
kitchen scale

medium bowl

handheld electric mixer

1 gallon resealable
plastic bag

rolling pin

sandwich spreader or
table knife

Makes
2 cups (enough to frost
24 cupcakes)

• • • • •
*This frosting is called
a buttercream frosting.
You can add small
amounts of melted
chocolate, citrus fruit
juice, instant coffee,
nuts, or vanilla extract
to it to give it a
distinctive flavor.*
• • • • •

*Find the diameter and radius of the top
of the medium bowl by using the
procedure from the Math Activity.*

Ingredients

½ cup (1 stick) margarine,
softened at room
temperature for 1 hour

½ pound confectioner's sugar

½ teaspoon salt

½ teaspoon vanilla extract

3 tablespoons 1% milk

½ pound confectioner's sugar

½ cup chopped walnuts
(optional)

Steps

1. Put the margarine, ½ pound confectioner's sugar, salt, and vanilla extract into the medium bowl. Beat with the electric mixer on medium speed until the mixture is creamy.

2. Add the milk and the remaining ½ pound confectioner's sugar and beat 1 to 2 minutes on medium speed until creamy. If too thick, add 1 more tablespoon milk.

3. If using walnuts, place them in the plastic bag and press out the excess air before closing. Rolling the rolling pin back and forth over the walnuts until they are finely crushed.

4. Use the sandwich spreader or table knife to ice cupcakes or cake of your choice. If you like, sprinkle with crushed walnuts.

···· Chocolate-Berry Shortcake ····

This recipe uses 9-inch pans, meaning that the diameter of each pan is 9 inches. What is the radius of each pan? Check Appendix A for the answer.

This fancy-looking two-layer cake is great to make when fresh strawberries are available.

Ingredients

vegetable oil cooking spray

¾ cup (1½ sticks) margarine, softened at room temperature for 1 hour

1⅔ cups sugar

3 eggs

1 teaspoon vanilla extract

2 cups all-purpose flour

⅔ cup cocoa powder

1¼ teaspoon baking soda

¼ teaspoon baking powder

1 teaspoon salt

1⅓ cups water

12 whole strawberries

¾ cup strawberry preserves

1½ cups any flavor ready-to-use frosting or Hint O'Berry Frosting (page 142)

Steps

1. Preheat the oven to 350°F.

2. Spray the cake pans with vegetable oil cooking spray.

3. In a large bowl, use the electric mixer at medium speed to mix together the margarine and sugar until the mixture is a light yellow color.

4. Add the eggs and vanilla extract, and beat at high speed for 3 to 4 minutes or until the mixture is smooth.

5. In the other large bowl, use the wooden spoon to stir together the flour, cocoa, baking soda, baking powder, and salt. Mix well.

Time
30 minutes to prepare
plus
30 to 35 minutes to bake
plus
130 minutes cooling time

Tools
2 round 9-inch cake pans

2 large bowls

spatula

electric mixer

wooden spoon

oven mitts

cooling rack

paring knife

strawberry huller

cutting board

serving plate

sandwich spreader or table knife

Makes
1 9-inch, 2-layer cake

6. Add some of the flour mixture, then some of the water, to the butter mixture. Mix with the electric mixer on low speed. Continue to add and mix until all the flour mixture and water are mixed in to the butter mixture. Mix for 2 minutes, or until all of the ingredients are well combined.

7. Pour the batter into the sprayed cake pans. Gently spread the batter with a sandwich spreader or table knife until the batter is level in each pan.

8. Bake the cakes for 30 to 35 minutes. Use oven mitts to remove the pans from the oven. To test for doneness, press the cake lightly in the center with your finger. If done, the cake should spring back. If not, put them back in the oven and test again in 3 minutes.

9. When the cakes are done, use oven mitts to remove the pans from the oven. Cool the cakes for 10 minutes.

10. Remove the cakes from the pans by turning the pans upside down on the cooling rack. Allow the cakes to cool for 2 hours.

11. Wash and dry the strawberries. Remove the strawberry stems with a paring knife or strawberry huller.

12. On the cutting board, slice 8 of the strawberries. Cut about ¼ inch off the wide end of each of the remaining 4 strawberries so that they will be able to stand upright.

13. Place one of the cakes on the serving plate. Use the sandwich spreader or table knife to spread the strawberry preserves on top of the cake.

14. Place the strawberry slices around the outer edge of the cake.

15. Place the second cake on top of the first cake.

16. Frost the top layer using ready-to-use frosting or Hint O'Berry Frosting. Do not frost the sides of the cakes.

17. Stand the whole strawberries in the center of the top of the cake. Decorate the cake with the remaining sliced strawberries.

•••••••••••••• ••••Hint O'Berry Frosting•••• •••••••••••

Time
10 minutes

Tools
kitchen scale

medium bowl

electric mixer

sandwich spreader or
table knife

Makes
1 cup frosting
(enough to frost the top of a
layer cake or 12 cupcakes)

• • • • •
*Food coloring is an edible
dye used to color foods.*
• • • • •

*Use the procedure from the Math Activity
to find the diameter and radius of the
bottom of the medium bowl.*

Ingredients

¼ cup (½ stick) margarine,
softened at room
temperature for 1 hour

½ pound confectioner's sugar

¼ teaspoon salt

1 teaspoon almond extract

2 tablespoons 1% milk

4 to 5 drops red food coloring

Steps

1. Put the margarine, ¼ pound confectioner's sugar, salt,
and almond extract into the medium bowl. Beat with
the electric mixer at medium speed until the mixture is
creamy.

2. Add the milk and the remaining ¼ pound confectioner's
sugar. Beat 1 to 2 minutes at medium speed until
creamy. If too thick, add 1 more tablespoon milk.

3. Add 4 to 5 drops of red food coloring. Continue to
beat at medium speed 1 more minute until the food
coloring is evenly blended into the frosting.

4. Use the sandwich spreader or table knife to frost the
top of the cake or twelve cupcakes of your choice.

······ ···· Grasshopper Ice Cream Tartlets ···· ·······

This recipe uses 4-inch pie crust, meaning that the diameter of each tart will be 4 inches or 100 millimeters in metric units. What is the tart's radius in millimeters? Check Appendix A for the answer.

*A **tart** is a single-serving pie that is usually made without a top crust. Larger pies are also called tarts. Tartlets refer only to single-serving pies.*

Ingredients

1 pint reduced-fat mint chocolate chip ice cream

1 package of 6 individual graham cracker pie crusts **(4-inch diameter)**

chocolate sauce

Steps

1. Scoop the ice cream into the large bowl.

2. Thaw the ice cream in the refrigerator for approximately 2 hours until it is soft but not liquid.

3. Spoon an even amount of ice cream into each graham cracker crust. Use the sandwich spreader or table knife to smooth the top of the ice cream.

4. Cover each graham cracker crust loosely with aluminum foil. Place on a cookie sheet.

5. Place the cookie sheet of tartlets in the freezer and freeze for at least 4 hours or until you are ready to serve.

6. Drizzle with chocolate sauce before serving.

Time
10 minutes to prepare
plus
6 hours for thawing and refreezing

Tools
large bowl

serving spoon

sandwich spreader or table knife

aluminum foil

cookie sheet

Makes
6 tartlets

CHAPTER 14

WHAT'S THE CIRCUMFERENCE OF A PIE?

The distance around a circle is called its circumference. The **circumference** of any circle divided by its diameter always equals approximately 3.14. The symbol for 3.14 is the Greek letter π, pronounced pi. The circumference of a circle is equal to π times the diameter of the circle, or $C = \pi \times d$. This formula is used below to calculate circumference.

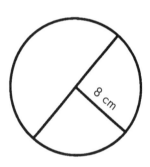

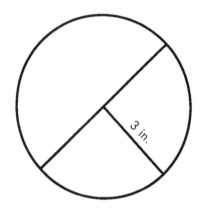

Radius	= 8 cm
Diameter	= 2 × 8 cm = 16 cm
Circumference	= $\pi \times d$
	= 3.14 × 16 cm
	= 50.24 cm

Radius	= 3 in.
Diameter	= 2 × 3 in. = 6 in
Circumference	= $\pi \times d$
	= 3.14 × 6 in.
	= 18.84 in.

The area of a circle is also calculated using π. The area of a circle is the amount of space inside a circle. The area of a circle is equal to π times the radius times the radius. That's $\pi \times r \times r$. This formula can be shortened to πr^2. The number 2 is an exponent, which indicates that the radius is being multiplied by itself. The calculations below show how to calculate the area of a circle.

$$\begin{aligned} \text{Area} &= \pi r^2 \\ &= 3.14 \times 8^2 \\ &= 3.14 \times 64 \\ &= 200.96 \text{ sq cm} \end{aligned} \qquad \begin{aligned} \text{Area} &= \pi r^2 \\ &= 3.14 \times 3^2 \\ &= 3.14 \times 9 \\ &= 28.26 \text{ sq in.} \end{aligned}$$

Pies that you eat are measured by their diameters. Therefore, when you get a 9-inch pie, it means the diameter is 9 inches. Round pans, such as those for making cakes and pies, are also specified by their diameters. Common sizes for these pans are 8 or 9 inches. Do the Math Activity to practice your pi-making skills.

PI PLEASURE

MATH ACTIVITY

Materials
two formulas
pencil
notebook

Procedure

1. Use the formulas to calculate the circumference and area of the following cookies. Write your calculations and answers in your notebook.

  a. A chocolate chip walnut cookie with a 4-inch diameter.

  b. A peanut butter oatmeal cookie with a 6-inch diameter.

2. Use the formulas to calculate the circumference and area of the following pancakes. Write your calculations and answers in your notebook.

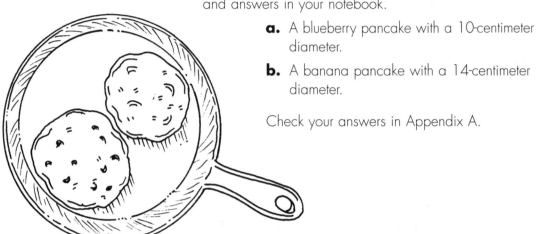

> **a.** A blueberry pancake with a 10-centimeter diameter.
>
> **b.** A banana pancake with a 14-centimeter diameter.
>
> Check your answers in Appendix A.

PIE RECIPES

Before you begin each of these recipes, calculate the circumference and area of the pie.

This recipe uses a prepared dough, called puff pastry dough, that you can find in the freezer section of the supermarket. Using this dough, you will make individual round tarts.

Before you start the recipe, draw a 3-inch-diameter circle and a 4-inch-diameter circle on a piece of posterboard or heavy paper. Cut out your circles. You will need these patterns to cut out round circles of dough for your apple tarts. The 4-inch circle will be the bottom crust for the tarts. Calculate the circumference and area of a 4-inch tart. Check your answers in Appendix A.

Time
45 minutes to prepare
plus
20 minutes to bake

Tools
cookie sheet

peeler

cutting board

apple corer

paring knife

medium frying pan

wooden spoon

rolling pin

custard cup or small bowl

fork

pastry brush

large spoon

small bowl

oven mitts

Makes
4 apple tarts

Ingredients

vegetable oil cooking spray

3 Granny Smith or other tart apples

2 tablespoons margarine

¼ cup light brown sugar

1 teaspoon vanilla extract

½ teaspoon cinnamon

1 tablespoon flour

1 package frozen prepared puff pastry dough, thawed at room temperature for ½ hour

1 egg

1 teaspoon water

2 teaspoons sugar

¼ teaspoon cinnamon

Steps

1. Preheat the oven to 350°F.

2. Spray the cookie sheet with vegetable oil cooking spray.

3. Wash and dry the apples, then peel them with the vegetable peeler.

4. On the cutting board, use the apple corer to remove the cores from the apples.

• • • • •
Puff pastry dough is made from the same ingredients as pie pastry— flour, salt, water, and butter—but it contains much more butter.
• • • • •

5. Use the paring knife to cut the apples in half, then cut the halves into thin slices.

6. Preheat the frying pan by placing it on a burner set to medium heat for 2 minutes.

7. Melt the margarine in the pan.

8. Add the apples, brown sugar, vanilla extract, and ½ teaspoon cinnamon to the pan and stir well with the wooden spoon.

9. Sauté the apples for about 5 to 8 minutes or until they are tender. Turn off the heat and set the pan aside until Step 15.

10. Sprinkle 1 tablespoon of flour on the cutting board or other clean surface. Use the rolling pin to roll out 1 sheet of the puffed pastry dough.

11. Using the 4-inch circle pattern and the paring knife, cut 8 4-inch circles out of the pastry dough.

12. Place the 3-inch circle pattern on top of one of the 4-inch circles. Cut around it with a paring knife. Remove the center of the dough and keep the dough ring. Do this 3 more times to make a total of 4 dough rings.

13. Break the egg in the custard cup or small bowl, beat the egg and the water together with the fork.

14. Use the pastry brush to lightly brush the egg mixture onto the 4 solid dough circles. These will become the bottoms of the apple tarts.

15. Use the large spoon to place 2 tablespoons of the apple mixture in the center of each solid circle.

16. Place a dough ring over the apple mixture on each of the solid dough circles. Use your fingers to press the edges of the top pastry lightly into the edges of bottom pastry. Use the prongs of the fork to seal the edges together.

17. Brush the sealed edges with the egg and water mixture.

18. In a small bowl, mix together the sugar and ¼ teaspoon cinnamon. Sprinkle the cinnamon sugar over the apples.

19. Place the 4 apple tarts on the sprayed cookie sheet.

20. Bake for 18 to 20 minutes, or until the pastry becomes puffy and a light golden brown color.

21. Use oven mitts to remove the cookie sheet from the oven. Cool for 10 minutes before serving.

···· Microwave Cherry Crisp ····

Time
25 minutes

Tools
**8-inch
(200-millimeter)
round microwave-
safe dish**

small bowl

wooden spoon

2 table knives

oven mitts

Makes
6 servings

If you want to make something quick and easy, try this recipe. But first, calculate the circumference and area of the microwave-safe dish. Check your answers in Appendix A.

Ingredients

1 21-ounce can cherry pie filling

1 teaspoon almond extract

¼ cup rolled oats

¼ cup toasted coconut

2 tablespoons all-purpose flour

2 tablespoons brown sugar

½ teaspoon ground cinnamon

2 tablespoons margarine

Steps

1. Pour the cherry filling into the microwave-safe dish, and spread it evenly. Sprinkle with almond extract.

2. In the small bowl, combine the oats, coconut, flour, brown sugar, and cinnamon. Mix well with the wooden spoon.

3. Add the margarine. Hold a table knife in each hand and draw the knives across each other to cut the margarine into the dry ingredients. Keep cutting until the mixture is crumbly.

4. Sprinkle the oat mixture over the cherry filling.

5. Microwave uncovered on high for 4 to 5 minutes, or until the filling is hot and bubbly. Using oven mitts, give the dish a half turn after 2 minutes.

6. Use oven mitts to remove the dish from the microwave. Let stand for 5 minutes before serving.

ANSWERS TO THE MATH ACTIVITIES

CHAPTER 1. **Math Activity**

1. a. 1 yd   = .9 m licorice
    b. 1 ft   = 30 cm submarine sandwich
    c. 1 in.   = 25 mm ravioli

2. a. 2 tsp   = 10 ml vanilla extract
    b. ¼ c   = 60 ml half-and-half
    c. 1 qt   = 946 ml skim milk

3. a. 1 oz   = 28 g chocolate bar
    b. 1 lb   = 454 g ground turkey
    c. 2.2 lbs   = 1 kg hot dogs

Baked Crunchy Chicken Bites

2 Tbsp   = ? ml milk
1 Tbsp   = 15 ml
2 Tbsp   = 15 × 2 ml
2 Tbsp   = 30 ml milk

Superquick Stromboli Slices

¼ lb   = 113 g ham

Lean & Mean Open-Face Turkey Burger

1 lb   = 454 g ground turkey

McQuick Oven Fries

1 Tbsp   = 15 ml oil

Light Milkshakes

1 c   = 240 ml low-fat or skim milk

CHAPTER 2. **Math Activity**

1. a. 1 m   = 3.3 ft red licorice
    b. 2 cm   = ? in. cracker
         1 cm   = .4 in.
         2 cm   = .4 × 2 in.
         2 cm   = .8 in. cracker

c. 10 mm   = ? in. raisin
10 mm   = 1 cm
1 cm   = .4 in.
10 mm   = .4 in. raisin

2. a. 4 l   = 1.06 gal apple cider

b. 2 l   = ? qts soda
1 l   = 1.06 qts
2 l   = 1.06 × 2 qts
2 l   = 2.12 qts soda

c. 500 ml = 1.06 pts milk

3. a. 1 kg   = 2.2 lbs green beans

b. 500 g   = 1.1 lbs hamburger meat

c. 100 g   = 3.5 oz canned corn

Nutmeg Baking Powder Biscuits
340 g   = 12 oz all-purpose flour

Say "Cheese Please" Scones
120 ml   = ? c 2% milk
240 ml   = 1 c
240 ml ÷ 2 = 1 c ÷ 2
120 ml   = ½ c 2% milk

Chocolate Chip Super Scones
120 ml   = ½ c 2% milk

CHAPTER 4. **Math Activity**

a. 1 Tbsp	= 3 tsp		**g.** 1 l	= 1000 ml
b. 1 c	= 16 Tbsp		**h.** 1 Tbsp	= ½ fl oz
c. 1 pt	= 2 c		**i.** 1 c	= 8 fl oz
d. 1 qt	= 4 c		**j.** 1 pt	= 16 fl oz
e. 1 qt	= 2 pts		**k.** 1 qt	= 32 fl oz
f. 1 gal	= 4 qts		**l.** 1 gal	= 128 fl oz

Rib-Stickin' Chicken and Number Soup
4 c   = 1 qt chicken broth

Zippy Vegetable Soup with Mini-Bow-Tie Pasta

½ l   = ? ml water
1 l   = 1000 ml water
1 l ÷ 2   = 1000 ml ÷ 2
½ l   = 500 ml water

Corn-off-the-Cob Chowder

1 c   = 8 fl oz water

Mexican Jumpin' Bean Soup

2 c   = 1 pt water

Melon Soup

1 c   = ? pt pineapple juice
2 c   = 1 pt
2 c ÷ 2 = 1 pt ÷ 2
1 c   = ½ pt pineapple juice

CHAPTER 5. **Math Activity**

4. **a.** 14 lb
   b. 4 oz
   c. 4 kg

CHAPTER 6. **Math Activity**

1. **a.** 78°F
   b. 15°F
   c. 6°C
   d. 27°C
2. **a.** warm soup
   b. ice cream

CHAPTER 7. **Math Activity**

1. **a.** 2×2 = 4 lb carrots
   b. 6×2 = 12 eggs
   c. 5×2 = 10 oz Swiss cheese
   d. 12×2 = 24 grapes

2. a. 3×3 = 9 c bread flour
  b. 2×3 = 6 tsp salt
  c. 4×3 = 12 apples
  d. 6×3 = 18 Tbsp buttermilk

Three-Cheese Grilled Cheese Sandwich

1×2 = 2 Tbsp low-fat mayonnaise dressing
2×2 = 4 slices whole wheat bread
1×2 = 2 slices American cheese
1×2 = 2 slices Muenster chese
1×2 = 2 slices Swiss cheese
3×2 = 6 pickle chips

Dinnertime California Burger in a Pocket

2×3 = 6 tomato slices
1×3 = 3 lettuce leaves
4×3 = 12 oz lean ground beef
1×3 = 3 dashes salt
1×3 = 3 dashes pepper
2×3 = 6 slices onion
1×3 = 3 pita breads
2×3 = 6 Tbsp low-fat mayonnaise dressing

Tuna and Melted Cheese Croissant Sandwich

4×4 = 16 Tbsp
2×4 = 8 Tbsp low-fat mayonnaise dressing

* * for 1 tsp dried chives, estimate about 2 tsp for 4 sandwiches

1×4 = 4 croissants
1×4 = 4 slices American cheese

* * The amount of dried chives does not get multiplied as do the other ingredients. Herbs and spices generally are not doubled, tripled, or quadrupled in recipes because that would be too much flavor! They are increased only slightly so they don't overpower the recipe.

CHAPTER 8. **Math Activity**

1. a. $6 \div 2$ = 3 eggs
    b. $4 \div 2$ = 2 apples
    c. $1 \div 2$ = ½ Tbsp (1½ tsp) parsley
    d. $12 \div 2$ = 6 grapes
2. a. $4 \div 4$ = 1 c bread flour
    b. $8 \div 4$ = 2 tsp sugar
    c. $16 \div 4$ = 4 ravioli
    d. $20 \div 4$ = 5 crackers

Baked Golden Apples and Carrots

For 2 servings:

$4 \div 4$ = 1 medium Golden Delicious apple
$12 \div 4$ = 3 carrots
$4 \div 4$ = 1 Tbsp brown sugar
$½ \div 4$ = 1 dash nutmeg
$8 \div 4$ = 2 tsp margarine

Cherry-Baked Apples

For 2 servings:

$6 \div 3$ = 2 apples
$9 \div 3$ = 3 Tbsp cherry pie filling
$12 \div 3$ = 4 fl oz cherry soda
$1 \div 3$ = ⅓ c water
$18 \div 3$ = 6 pecan pieces

Starburst Apple English Muffins

For 2 servings:

$2 \div 2$ = 1 small apple
$4 \div 2$ = 2 English muffins
$8 \div 2$ = 4 Tbsp light cream cheese
$8 \div 2$ = 4 Tbsp raisins
$2 \div 2$ = 1 tsp cinnamon
$2 \div 2$ = 1 tsp sugar

CHAPTER 9. **Fresh Fruit Platter with Yummy Yogurt Dip**

4 servings: about 2 c of sliced fruit
6 servings: about 3 c of sliced fruit

Tortilla 'n' Cheese Fiesta Salad

4 servings:
  about 6 c romaine lettuce
  about 8 to 12 tomato slices
  about 16 tortilla chips
  about 4 olives
  about ½ c shredded sharp cheddar cheese

6 servings:
  about 9 c romaine lettuce
  about 12 to 18 tomato slices
  about 24 tortilla chips
  about 6 olives
  about ¾ c shredded sharp cheddar cheese

CHAPTER 10. Math Activity

1. a. 1¾ + ¼ = 1⁴⁄₄ = 2 c brown sugar
  b. ¾ + ¼ = ⁴⁄₄ = 1 tsp vanilla extract
  c. ½ + ½ = ²⁄₂ = 1 tsp salt
  d. 2 + 2½ = 4½ c all-purpose flour

Hiking Munchies

1¼ + ¾ = 1⁴⁄₄ = 2 c low-fat granola cereal

Fraction Pretzels

⅔ + ⅔ = ⁴⁄₃ = 1⅓ c lukewarm water

Lunch-Box Granola

⅕ + ⅘ = ⁵⁄₅ = 1 c rolled oats

Peachy Snack Rolls

9 + 1½ = 10½ oz frozen peaches

CHAPTER 11. Math Activity

Percent of margarine $\dfrac{2\ c}{9\ c}$ = .22 × 100 = 22%

Banana Blaster Muffins

Percent of chocolate chips $\dfrac{1\ c}{3\ c}$ = .33 × 100 = 33%

Munchin' Crunchin' Butterscotch Muffins

Percent of butterscotch morsels $\dfrac{1\ c}{3\ c}$ = .33 × 100 = 33%

CHAPTER 12. Math Activity

1. **a.** 18 in. × 26 in. = 468 sq in.
    b. 46 cm × 66 cm = 3036 sq cm
    c. 12 in. × 20 in. = 240 sq in.
    d. 13 in. × 18 in. = 234 sq in.

Double-Cool Brownie and Cream Bars

9 in. × 9 in. = 81 sq in.

Rectangle Cheesecake Snacks

9 in. × 9 in. = 81 sq in.

Cinnamon Strawberry Breakfast Squares

9 in. × 13 in. = 117 sq in.

Luscious Lemon Squares

8 in. × 8 in. = 64 sq in.

Microwave Butterscotch Applesauce Bars

200 mm × 200 mm = 40,000 sq mm

CHAPTER 13. Math Activity

a. diameter = 10 in.

radius $= \dfrac{d}{2}$

radius $= \dfrac{10}{2}$

radius = 5 in.

b. radius = 3 cm
diameter = 2r
diameter = 2 × 3
diameter = 6 cm

Chocolate-Berry Shortcake

diameter = 9 in.

radius $= \dfrac{d}{2}$

radius $= \dfrac{9}{2}$

radius $= 4\frac{1}{2}$ in.

Grasshopper Ice Cream Tartlets

diameter = 100 mm

radius $= \dfrac{d}{2}$

radius $= \dfrac{100}{2}$

radius $= 50$ mm

CHAPTER 14. Math Activity

1. a. Chocolate chip walnut cookie

diameter = 4 in. radius = 2 in.

$C = \pi \times d$

$\quad = 3.14 \times 4$

$\quad = 12.56$ in.

$A = \pi r^2$

$\quad = 3.14 \times 2^2$

$\quad = 3.14 \times 4$

$\quad = 12.56$ sq in.

b. Peanut butter oatmeal cookie

diameter = 6 in. radius = 3 in.

$C = \pi \times d$

$\quad = 3.14 \times 6$

$\quad = 18.84$ in.

$A = \pi r^2$

$\quad = 3.14 \times 3^2$

$\quad = 3.14 \times 9$

$\quad = 28.26$ sq in.

2. a. Blueberry pancake

diameter = 10 cm radius = 5 cm

$C = \pi \times d$

$\quad = 3.14 \times 10$

$\quad = 31.4$ cm

$A = \pi r^2$

$\quad = 3.14 \times 5^2$

$\quad = 3.14 \times 25$

$\quad = 78.5$ sq cm

b. Banana pancake

diameter = 14 cm radius = 7 cm

$C = \pi \times d$

$\quad = 3.14 \times 14$

$\quad = 43.96$ cm

$A = \pi r^2$

$\quad = 3.14 \times 7^2$

$\quad = 3.14 \times 49$

$\quad = 153.86$ sq cm

Apples in the Round

4-in. tart diameter = 4 in. radius = 2 in.

$C = \pi \times d$

$\quad = 3.14 \times 4$ in.

$\quad = 12.56$ in.

$A = \pi r^2$

$\quad = 3.14 \times 2^2$ in.

$\quad = 3.14 \times 4$ in.

$\quad = 12.56$ sq in.

Microwave Cherry Crisp

200-mm round dish diameter = 200 mm

radius = 100 mm

$C = \pi \times d$

    $= 3.14 \times 200$ mm

    $= 628$ mm

$A = \pi r^2$

    $= 3.14 \times 100^2$ mm

    $= 3.14 \times 10{,}000$ mm

    $= 31{,}400$ sq mm

NUTRIENT CONTENT OF RECIPES

This table shows the amount of calories, fat, cholesterol, fiber, and sodium contained in one serving of each recipe in this book. You can compare these numbers to how much you need daily as described in Appendix C.

Recipe	Serving Size	Calories	Fat (grams)	Cholesterol (milligrams)	Fiber (grams)	Sodium (milligrams)
Chapter 1						
Baked Crunchy Chicken Bites	⅙ recipe	222	9	56	1	178
Superquick Stromboli Slices	⅛ slice	384	20	54	0	909
Lean & Mean Open-Face Turkey Burger	1 burger	320	14	83	2	487
McQuick Oven Fries	⅙ recipe	117	4	0	2	361
Light Milkshakes	1 cup	194	5	18	0	124
Chapter 2						
Nutmeg Baking Powder Biscuits	1 biscuit	117	4	0	0	221
Say "Cheese Please" Scones	1 scone	169	11	31	0	266
Chocolate Chip Super Scones	1 scone	340	19	40	1	360
Chapter 3						
Giant Oatmeal Raisin Chocolate Chip Cookies	1 cookie	294	13	13	2	174

Recipe	Serving Size	Calories	Fat (grams)	Cholesterol (milligrams)	Fiber (grams)	Sodium (milligrams)
Speckled Peanut Butter Chewies	1 cookie	96	5	7	1	65
Lemon Drop Sugar Cookies	1 cookie	96	5	6	0	79
Awesome Animal Crackers	1 cracker	88	4	10	0	150
Taste-of-Honey Spread	1 tablespoon	90	8	0	0	102
Microwave Chocolate Walnut Cookies	1 cookie	93	6	7	0	110

Chapter 4

Recipe	Serving Size	Calories	Fat (grams)	Cholesterol (milligrams)	Fiber (grams)	Sodium (milligrams)
Rib-Stickin' Chicken and Number Soup	1½ cups	395	17	105	4	965
Zippy Vegetable Soup with Mini-Bow-Tie Pasta	1½ cups	349	8	0	6	693
Corn-off-the-Cob Chowder	1½ cups	423	12	29	10	1006
Mexican Jumpin' Bean Soup	1½ cups	330	18	39	3	860
Melon Soup	1 cup	95	0	1	1	20

Chapter 5

Recipe	Serving Size	Calories	Fat (grams)	Cholesterol (milligrams)	Fiber (grams)	Sodium (milligrams)
Fantastic Fettuccine	1 cup	438	22	62	0	760
Zero Meat Tomato Sauce	½ cup	72	6	0	1	115
Garden Tomato and Basil Sauce	½ cup	110	9	5	1	124
Scooped Tomatoes Stuffed with Tuna Pasta Salad	1 tomato	286	8	20	2	535

Recipe	Serving Size	Calories	Fat (grams)	Cholesterol (milligrams)	Fiber (grams)	Sodium (milligrams)
Chapter 6						
Caramel Candy Cubes	1½-ounce piece	96	4	3	0	63
Mallo-Mallo Fudge Squares	1 piece	168	8	3	0	68
Brown Sugar Turtle Pralines	1 piece	143	8	9	1	19
Chapter 7						
Three-Cheese Grilled Cheese Sandwich	1 sandwich	356	20	40	7	862
Dinnertime California Burger in a Pocket	1 sandwich	369	20	56	1	591
Tuna and Melted Cheese Croissant Sandwich	1 sandwich	358	20	49	1	896
Chapter 8						
Baked Golden Apples and Carrots	½ cup	146	4	0	5	91
Cherry-Baked Apples	1 apple	187	7	0	4	10
Starburst Apple English Muffins	2 muffin halves	335	11	31	4	446
Chapter 10						
Hiking Munchies	½ cup	424	22	0	4	669
Fraction Pretzels	2 pretzels	138	2	18	2	539
Lunch-Box Granola	½ cup	206	10	0	2	22
Peachy Snack Rolls	1 roll	36	0	0	1	2
Chapter 11						
Banana Blaster Muffins	1 muffin	250	11	20	2	325
Whole Wheat Honey and Date Muffins	1 muffin	220	9	18	3	263

Recipe	Serving Size	Calories	Fat (grams)	Cholesterol (milligrams)	Fiber (grams)	Sodium (milligrams)
PB & J Surprise Muffins	1 muffin	227	10	18	2	298
Radical Peach Muffins	1 muffin	183	7	18	2	313
Munchin' Crunchin' Butterscotch Muffins	1 muffin	267	15	20	2	359
Chapter 12						
Double-Cool Brownie and Cream Bars	1 piece (1/18 of recipe)	288	16	53	0	298
Rectangle Cheesecake Snacks	1 piece (1/18 of recipe)	178	12	27	0	93
Cinnamon Strawberry Breakfast Squares	1 piece (1/12 of recipe)	429	25	18	2	237
Luscious Lemon Squares	1 piece (1/16 of recipe)	132	5	27	0	130
Microwave Butterscotch Applesauce Bars	1 piece (1/12 of recipe)	162	6	9	1	40
Chapter 13						
Nutty Carrot-Top Cupcakes, unfrosted	1 cupcake	286	17	27	1	171
Ultimate Butternut Frosting	2 tablespoons	80	3	8	0	63
Chocolate-Berry Shortcake, unfrosted	1 slice (1/12 of recipe)	359	15	53	1	460
Hint O'Berry Frosting	2 tablespoons	80	3	8	0	63
Grasshopper Ice Cream Tartlets	1 tartlet	280	12	20	1	190
Chapter 14						
Apples in the Round	1 tart	296	13	53	2	115
Microwave Cherry Crisp	1 slice (1/6 of recipe)	194	7	0	0	73

NUTRITION IN A NUTSHELL

Nutrition is about you and food. It is the food you eat and how the body uses it. You need food to get energy to play, to breathe, and to keep your heart beating. The energy in food is called **calories.** Food also provides a variety of substances called **nutrients** that are needed to help you grow, to repair your body, and to keep you healthy.

A booklet from the U.S. Department of Agriculture and the U.S. Department for Health and Human Services called *Dietary Guidelines for Americans* provides the following answers to the question "What should we be eating to stay healthy?"

1. *Eat a variety of foods.* You need more than 40 different nutrients for good health.

2. *Maintain a healthy weight.* If you are too fat or too thin, your chances of developing health problems are increased. To lose weight, you need to eat fewer calories (calories tell us how much energy is packed in each food).

3. *Choose a diet low in fat and cholesterol.* **Fat** is a nutrient that supplies more energy than any other nutrient. People who eat diets high in fat are more likely to have heart disease and certain types of cancer than people who don't. Some fats you eat you can actually see—such as margarine, vegetable oil, and butter. But many other fats are not so obvious—such as the fat in hamburgers, in whole milk and many cheeses, in cookies, cakes, fried foods, mayonnaise, salad dressings, and other foods. **Cholesterol** is a fatlike nutrient made in the body and found in every cell. Eggs and liver contain the highest amounts of cholesterol found in foods.

4. *Eat plenty of vegetables, fruits, and grain products, such as breads, cereals, pasta, and rice.* These foods are generally low in fats. By choosing them often, you are likely to decrease fats and increase **carbohydrates** in your diet. Carbohydrates are a group of nutrients that include sugar, starch, and **fiber**. Fiber is found only in plant foods such as fruits, vegetables, and grains. Eating fiber has many desirable effects.

5. *Don't use a lot of sugar.* Sugars and foods that contain them in large amounts supply calories but few nutrients. Therefore, people don't need much sugar and it can add unnecessary weight.

6. *Don't use a lot of salt and sodium.* Table salt contains sodium and chlorine—two minerals needed in your diet. However, most Americans eat more salt and sodium than they need. Sodium is also added to a lot of foods during processing. Always check labels carefully before you buy.

THE FOOD GUIDE PYRAMID

Another way to look at what we need to eat each day is pictured in the accompanying illustration, the Food Guide Pyramid. The Food Guide Pyramid emphasizes foods from the five food groups shown in the three lower sections. Each of these food groups provides some, but not all, of the nutrients you need. Foods in one group can't replace those in another. No one food group is more important than another—for good health, you need them all. But you need more of some groups, such as bread, than others, such as fats. Also, vary your choices of foods within each group, because specific foods differ in the kinds and amounts of nutrients they provide.

The Food Guide Pyramid
A Guide to Daily Food Choices

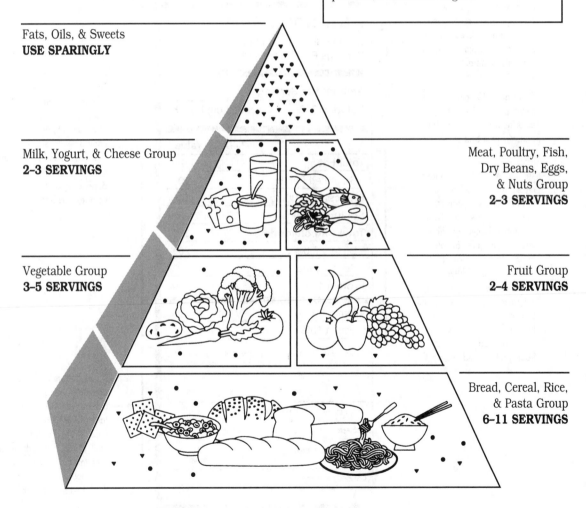

Fats, Oils, & Sweets
USE SPARINGLY

Milk, Yogurt, & Cheese Group
2–3 SERVINGS

Meat, Poultry, Fish,
Dry Beans, Eggs,
& Nuts Group
2–3 SERVINGS

Vegetable Group
3–5 SERVINGS

Fruit Group
2–4 SERVINGS

Bread, Cereal, Rice,
& Pasta Group
6–11 SERVINGS

HOW TO READ A FOOD LABEL

Ever notice that little section of the food label called Nutrition Facts on the foods you buy at the supermarket? Let's check it out—from top to bottom—on a frozen dinner.

The serving size is 12 ounces—that's ¾ pound. This package has 1 serving in it, so you'd have to eat all the food in the package to get the amounts of the nutrients listed.

There are 340 calories in the serving, and 45 of those calories come from fat. That doesn't seem bad at all.

The nutrients listed are those most important to the health of the average American. You should try to eat 100% of your carbohydrate, fiber, vitamin, and mineral values in one day, over several meals. You should keep down the percentage of fat, saturated fat, cholesterol, and sodium. This food is not too high in fat and cholesterol and is a good source of fiber, protein, and vitamin C.

The % Daily Value column tells you how much of the daily recommended amount of a nutrient this food contributes to a 2,000-calorie diet. Your daily values may be higher or lower depending on how many calories you need.

At the bottom of the label are listed the recommended amounts of various nutrients for a 2,000- and a 2,500-calorie diet. For fat, cholesterol, and sodium, the amounts are maximums— you should try to eat *less* than the listed amounts.

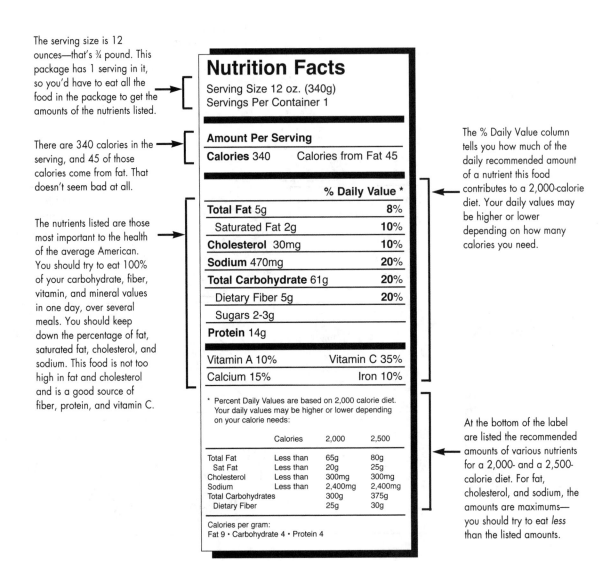

Nutrition Facts

Serving Size 12 oz. (340g)
Servings Per Container 1

Amount Per Serving

Calories 340   Calories from Fat 45

% Daily Value *

Total Fat 5g	**8%**
Saturated Fat 2g	**10%**
Cholesterol 30mg	**10%**
Sodium 470mg	**20%**
Total Carbohydrate 61g	**20%**
Dietary Fiber 5g	**20%**
Sugars 2-3g	
Protein 14g	

Vitamin A 10%	Vitamin C 35%
Calcium 15%	Iron 10%

* Percent Daily Values are based on 2,000 calorie diet. Your daily values may be higher or lower depending on your calorie needs:

		Calories	2,000	2,500
Total Fat	Less than		65g	80g
Sat Fat	Less than		20g	25g
Cholesterol	Less than		300mg	300mg
Sodium	Less than		2,400mg	2,400mg
Total Carbohydrates			300g	375g
Dietary Fiber			25g	30g

Calories per gram:
Fat 9 • Carbohydrate 4 • Protein 4

APPENDIX D

WHAT'S SAFE TO EAT?

Even if you choose a very nutritious diet, there are still dangers lurking in your food. They seem to be reported on television and in the newspapers and magazines all the time. Are apples really sprayed with a dangerous chemical? Is eating an undercooked fast-food hamburger going to hospitalize you? Let's look at how to keep food safe.

FOOD POISONING

Foodborne illness, commonly called food poisoning, is caused by substances in food, such as bacteria and molds, which make you sick to your stomach but can be even more serious. Sometimes fever and infection occur. The symptoms may start within an hour of eating the suspected food or up to several days later.

Foodborne illness is most often caused by microorganisms. Microorganisms include bacteria and viruses. *Micro* means small, and both bacteria and viruses are so small that they cannot be seen by the naked eye. Bacteria are in the air, in the ground, and on you and me. Given the right temperature and enough time, bacteria will multiply in food (they double in number every 20 minutes). Bacteria cause foodborne illness when they multiply in food to the point that when the food is eaten, they make you very sick. Luckily, not all bacteria cause foodborne illness; only a small number do.

Bacteria grow readily under these three conditions.

1. **In a food that contains some protein,** such as meat, poultry, fish, eggs, dairy products, gravies and sauces, potatoes, beans, and rice.

2. **At a temperature between 40°F and 140°F.** Refrigeration is normally at or below 45° F, so bacteria grow slowly if at all. Bacterial growth slows down even more in the freezer, which is usually kept at or below 0°F. Room temperature is normally around 70°F—a great temperature for bacteria to grow.

3. For at least 2 hours in the temperature zone given in # 2.

In some, but not all, cases, adequate cooking of the contaminated food (to 165°F) will prevent problems. However, cooking does not kill all forms of bacteria, and in many cases the contaminated food may not even be cooked further, as in the case of tuna salad.

Here are some ways to prevent foodborne illness in your home.

1. Keep hot foods hot and cold foods cold (below 45°F).

2. Wash your hands frequently, especially after handling raw meat, poultry, seafood, or eggs.

3. Don't touch yourself while handling food, because bacteria on your skin can then be introduced into the food. Don't use your fingers to taste food—use a spoon.

4. Cover all cuts, burns, and boils with a waterproof bandage. Cuts, burns, and boils are the home to many bacteria that you don't want in your food.

5. Keep all equipment sparkling clean and wash after every use. For instance, if you use your cutting board for cutting chicken, wash it thoroughly with *hot* water and soap before cutting lettuce on it (wash your knife, too)!

6. Use a different spoon for stirring raw foods, such as meat that is being browned, and cooked foods.

7. Cook and reheat foods until they are very hot and well done.

8. Don't eat raw meat, fish, or eggs. They may contain harmful bacteria, viruses, or parasites. If a dough or batter contains raw eggs, don't eat it before it is cooked!

9. Thaw meats, poultry, and seafood in the refrigerator overnight. Don't leave them out to thaw.

These are good rules to follow. A final rule of thumb is: "When in doubt, throw it out." It's probably not worth getting sick over.

MOLDS

Ever notice a little bluish green fuzz growing on your tomatoes? You probably knew it was just mold, but wondered if you could just cut out the moldy spot or if you should throw out the entire tomato. Molds cause spoilage (most often of fruits and bread), musty odors, and yucky flavors in foods. Molds also grow on vegetables, meats, and cheese that have been exposed to the air. Although molds will be killed by most cooking, the toxins (poisons) they produce will not, so you need to avoid eating moldy food. In foods with a firm texture, such as potatoes and hard cheeses, you can just cut out the moldy area. When dealing with a soft food, such as bread or tomatoes, it is best to throw the food out if you find any mold on it.

To avoid a dangerous mold that grows on peanuts (and corn), it is best to buy national brands. Also, throw out any moldy peanuts, peanut butter, cornmeal, or other corn products.

PESTICIDES

Pesticides are chemicals used to control insects, diseases, weeds, fungi, mold, and other pests on plants, vegetables, fruits, and animals. Pesticides are normally applied to crops as a spray, fog, or dust.

The government allows a small amount of pesticides to be left on the food you buy, but to be safe, you should avoid eating them. Here's how.

- Buy organically grown fruits and vegetables (these are grown without the use of pesticides) when possible.
- Throw away the outer leaves of leafy vegetables such as lettuce.
- Wash fruits and vegetables carefully, using a brush.
- Peel carrots, waxed cucumbers, peaches, and pears, because these foods are more likely to have hazardous pesticide residues.
- Buy local produce, as it is probably treated with less pesticide than produce that has to travel a long distance.
- Trim fat and skin from meat, poultry, and fish. Pesticides in animal feed can concentrate in animal fat. Skim fat from pan drippings, broths, sauces, and soups.
- Eat a varied diet so that no one food dominates.

GLOSSARY

area The number of squares with sides equal to one unit contained in a shape; length times width.

baker's percents The amount of ingredients needed in a baking recipe that is expressed as a percentage of the amount of flour in the recipe.

beat To move a utensil back and forth to blend ingredients together.

blend To mix two or more ingredients thoroughly until uniform.

boil To be at the boiling point—212°F or 100°C for water. When a liquid boils, that means it is turning into steam (the gaseous state of water).

calorie A measure of the energy in food.

carbohydrate A group of nutrients that includes sugar, starch, and fiber.

celsius A temperature scale in which 0° represents the freezing point and 100° represents the boiling point of water.

cholesterol A fatlike nutrient made in the body and found in every cell.

chop To cut into irregularly sized pieces.

circumference The distance around a circle.

convert To change from one form to another.

cream To mix margarine or butter and sugar by pressing them against the bowl with the back of a spoon until they look creamy.

decimal A number with one or more places to the right of a decimal point, such as 2.5.

denominator The bottom number in a fraction.

diameter A line segment with both end points on the circle that passes through the center of the circle.

dice To cut into cubes of the same size.

estimate To calculate approximately.

factor The numbers that are multiplied.

fahrenheit A temperature scale in which 32° represents the freezing point and 212° represents boiling of water.

fat A nutrient that supplies more energy than any other nutrient.

fiber A variety of substances present in plant foods that can't be digested in the body.

firm-ball stage In candy making, syrup cooked to a temperature of 244° to 248°F. A drop of the syrup, when dropped into very cold water, forms a firm ball that does not flatten when removed from the water.

fold To mix ingredients using a gentle over-and-under motion with a utensil.

foodborne illness A disease caused by substances in food, such as bacteria or molds, that make you sick.

fraction A number that names part of a whole.

grate   To rub a food across a grater's tiny punched holes to product small or fine pieces of food.

improper fraction   A fraction in which the numerator is greater than the denominator.

knead   To work dough into a smooth mass by pressing and folding with your hands.

mince   To chop very fine.

mix   To combine ingredients so that they are all evenly distributed.

numerator   The top number in a fraction.

nutrient   One of many substances in food that are needed for you to grow, to repair your body, and to keep you healthy.

nutrition   The science that explores the food you eat and how the body uses it.

percent   A ratio that compares some number to 100.

pi   When the circumference of a circle is divided by its diameter, you always get the number 3.14, which is also called pi.

praline   A rich, patty-shaped candy made with sugar, cream, butter, and pecans.

product   The answer in a multiplication problem.

protein   A nutrient that is needed for your body to grow and be healthy.

radius   A line segment that joins the center of a circle with any point on the circle's edge.

ratio   A comparison of two related numbers.

sauté   To cook quickly in a pan over medium-high heat in a small amount of fat or liquid.

scone   A baked good similar to a biscuit, only richer in taste because the dough contains eggs, cream, or butter.

shred   To rub a food across a surface with medium to large holes or slits to produce small pieces of food.

simmer   To cook in a liquid that is just below boiling.

slice   To cut into uniform slices.

sodium   A mineral present in salt, which is needed by your body.

soft-ball stage   In candy making, syrup cooked to a temperature of 234° to 240°F. A drop of syrup, when dropped into very cold water, forms a soft ball that flattens when removed from the water.

tart   A single-serving pie that is usually made without a top crust. Larger pies are also sometimes called tarts.

volume   The amount of space taken up by a three-dimensional figure measured in cubic units.

whip   To beat rapidly using a circular motion, usually with a wire whip, to incorporate air into the mixture (such as in making whipped cream).

whisk   To beat ingredients together with a wire whip until they are well blended.

yeast   A tiny, singled-celled organism that makes bread dough rise.

INDEX